The Quest for Tru
Vision-based Le

Cover design by Matthew Helf and Amy Kohlenhoefer
Illustrations by Joe Anderson, PhD
Library of Congress Cataloging in Publication Data
Anderson, Joseph Vernon, 1950 –
The Quest for Truth & Glory: Vision-based Leadership /
Joe Anderson, PhD
ISBN - 978-0-9847120-1-4

1. Creativity. 2. Leadership. 3. Vision.
4. Business. 5. History. 6. Culture

Includes bibliographical references.

. . . . .

To Mssrs. Jefferson and Roosevelt.
You taught me how to live.

Contents

1

I HAD AN IDEA THE OTHER DAY ...

"I had an idea ..." That's how it starts. A single voice. A moment in time. Often, very soft - like a whispered spring breeze. And gone just as easily. But in that moment rests the tipping point of history. It is the origin of change. It is also the seed of leadership being planted.

Let's take a look at that, shall we?

Organizations live and die by their leaders. Good ones preside over growth, prosperity and victory. Bad ones drive them into the trash heap of history. And it doesn't matter whether the organization is a church, an army or Proctor and Gamble; leadership is the key to communal welfare. That's why we pay leaders the big bucks. It's also why we spend billions trying to discover, create, train and mold victorious, prosperous leaders.

- We devour books on how to *act* as a leader.
- We offer graduate degrees in how to *function* as a leader,
- and endless seminars on what to <u>do</u> as a leader,
- and when to do it, and to whom.

The result is a complex and convoluted network of processes, structures and steps; as though a secret algorithm or button can trigger the next Churchill or Einstein --- all based on what a leader <u>does.</u> But, contrary to this mountain of social convention and popular belief, let me suggest that …

Leadership is NOT just what you <u>do</u>. Instead, it is in large measure, *what you **are**.*

You have to BE a leader, not just act like one.
You have to BE the power source for the entire organization:

- Be the guide and mapper of direction
- Be the engine of urgency,
- Be the voice of inspiration,
- Be the task master and pay master
- and be the community cheerleader.

But none of those matter unless you are first and foremost the dreamer of dreams, possessor of "the idea". A leader, it turns out, is first and foremost a visionary. He has to know where B is.

Finding B

Leadership is conceptually a very simple thing - it is the ability to get a group to move from point A to point B. The problem is that most organizations do not know where the heck B is - because the leader doesn't know. They don't have vision - the ability to see clearly where the firm needs to be, and what it will take to get there. They lack the idea.

So instead, they focus on a number - the surest sign of a leadership vacuum.

> "Ok boys! Let's storm the ramparts! Get that 7% increase in sales! No vacations 'til we do. No more lollygagging! It's not the size of the dog in the fight, but the size of the fight in the dog. By god, we'll do it! Because when we do, well then hurrah and hallelujah! - we'll get to chase 8% next year. Won't that be grand?"

Chasing 7%, or 8% - or any number for that fact - is **_not_** an idea. It is a *substitute* for an idea. I can't think of anything else to get my folks to work together, so I'll make up a number to chase. It's better than nothing. But frankly, it amounts to chasing your tail. About the only thing that happens then, is the organization gets better and better at spinning its wheels.

But it *is* focused. And orderly. And aligned. And predictable. And efficient (oh Lord, does it get efficient). And it's driven by that old adage -- "If you can't measure it (put a number to it) you can't manage it. That's true. BUT - the firm's just not going anywhere. It's chasing its own tail for god's sake! Who gives a damn how *fast* it's going?

Let me suggest a New Adage: if you *can* measure it, you can't possibly lead it. You see, there's an intriguing difference between managing and leading. It's time to learn the latter.

Before we go any further, though, take a look in the psychic mirror. Is your organization chasing ideas, or numbers? Would you and the world be better served if you put a bit more emphasis on the ideas? That's what Vision-Based Leadership is all about: getting - and fighting for - a new idea.

B = The Idea

Simply put, an idea is the comprehension of something that *could* exist.

- If that thing is a tangible object or procedure we call it a concrete idea.
- If it is a value, belief, concept or opinion we call it an abstract idea.
- And if it is a progression of acts that will lead to the realization of that concrete or abstract idea, we call it a plan.

All well and good, but where does a leader get one of these ideas? Ah … now this gets us into the realm of tweed jackets, wine, cheese, and philosophy. It's the Nature versus Nurture debate.

- Some folks see man as a clean slate. Born with nothing. No values, no sense of right or wrong. No ability to reason. Nothing, Nada. Zip. So our ideas, and our ability to reason comes from Nurture - the people that surround us, and all the facts, passions and social conventions they pour into us.
- Other folks see man as arriving with a full kit: basic reasoning skills, a sense of right and wrong, the works. These innate abilities (instincts) are a gift of Nature. All we lack are specific facts.

Both parties to the argument, however, agree that individuals are rounded out by our contextual experience, our personal environment. That environment gives each of us a unique set of problems to solve and opportunities to exploit. And that

4

invites us to produce a new idea for dealing with our world. But, to produce that idea we've got to unleash our imagination.

Imagination

… is a marvel of fantasy, fact and reason. It is the process of forming a new idea that is not solely a reconstruction or extension of what has been experienced by the senses. And this freedom from the senses means that imagination is unfettered by objective restraints. Do you want a man who is

- capable of leaping over tall buildings in a single bound?
- More powerful than a locomotive?
- Faster that a speeding bullet?

No problem. Just unleash your imagination, and slap an "S" on his chest. Nothing is impossible in the imagination, which is why Einstein said, "Imagination ... is more important than knowledge. Knowledge is limited. Imagination encircles the world."

And all of this - Leadership. Vision, Ideas, Imagination - comes back to the concept of Creativity; the production of something original.

Vision-based Leadership cannot be separated from Creativity

- Without creativity you don't get the idea.
- Without the idea you don't have the vision.
- Without the vision you don't get B, because no one has the foggiest notion of where B is, or how to get there.

And if no one knows where B is, there can't - by definition - be a leader. All you have is a herd of sheep milling around with no place to go.

Here's the so what

It's getting harder and harder to come up with B - because of the amount of change that is swirling around us. You see, humanity imposes a self-limiting governor on its own creativity. That's because of the unconscious benefit/cost analysis humans perform relative to creativity and the rate of change in the environment.

- If you have an absolutely static environment (rate of change = 0), the brain just doesn't kick into gear. There are no new opportunities (no benefits) and no new problems (costs) - so there is no incentive to think and we roll over for yet another intellectual nap.

- But the environment does periodically change (rate of change = moderate) - via floods, famines, earthquakes, the accidental discovery of honey or fire - and when that happens the benefit/cost phenomena kicks into gear and humans get amazingly creative.

- However, all that human activity creates a rapid rate of change, in and of itself. And that drives the benefit/cost ratio to zero because no matter how good your ideas are, they're obsolete by the time you implement them. So why try? Once again, there is no incentive and humanity rolls over for yet another intellectual nap.

That's why technological and social changes occur in bunches. Somebody invents a steam engine, and we suddenly get real busy addressing the world's opportunities and problems. But those ideas, themselves, become part of the environment and that environment starts to change at an increasingly rapid rate - because of our ideas. And as that happens we actually start generating fewer ideas, due to the benefit/cost phenomena. And the rate of change calms back down. Then somebody invents a car, or a phone or an internet and BAM! all sorts of other ideas start popping; and the cycle repeats itself.

And right now we're living through one of those periods when the rate of change is over the moon. It's so hard to keep up that the natural inclination is to watch more reruns, play more computer games and take more naps. So now, more than ever, vision-based leadership needs our conscious focus and stimulus … not because humanity is dim or lazy, but because it has been so damn bright and busy.

Here's a 2nd so what - every new idea hits a wall.

Ask any U.S. president. They can't turn on the lights at the White House without rabid attacks from the opposing party. And it gets worse if the president actually tries to do something meaningful.

> Ask Jimmy Carter about switching America to the metric system, or Bush #2 about changing the way Medicare covers medications --- or Obama about improving the health of 40 million poor folks, so they can show up for minimum wage jobs each day, and thereby earn profits for the very people who were fighting against Obamacare.

Now, if the Commander in Chief of the World's most powerful nation takes it on the chin from his own people when he pursues an idea - which history will eventually tell us was a good one - then what do _you_ expect? You're just an average Joe: an entrepreneur, or a cog in someone else's corporate machinery; a spouse, parent, child or orphan. And it doesn't matter whether you occupy the C suite (CEO, CFO, CIO etc.) or some middle management job, you still have to pop out of bed and haul yourself into work with a can-do attitude because … well, by god … you are a leader.

Well take heart. You're not really the target. The idea is. Any new idea causes change, and change always triggers resistance. So sticking to your guns is a big part of being a leader. That's where moral fiber, persistence, and a strong left hook come into play. Walk softly, but carry a big stick.

Teddy Roosevelt said that. He was a visionary leader. Look in the mirror. Where's your stick? I'm thinkin' you're gonna need one.

OK - Let's summarize

Vision-based leadership is crucial to success in any endeavor, but it is among the first things to go when life gets complex. The solution is to consciously focus on two things:

1. Creativity - coming up with the new idea, and

2. Power - pursuing that idea in spite of resistance

Those two things are the focus of this book, especially the latter. We're going to immerse ourselves in the battle to bring ideas to fruition.

But first, let's get a few things straight

Albert Einstein never needed a book like this. Neither did Michelangelo nor da Vinci nor Steve Jobs for that matter. I'd also suggest that Steven Spielberg doesn't need it either. Because those folks are what I'd call "pure Creatives" – one-man idea factories. They're born with it. And it is utterly impossible to educate or train someone to be a pure Creative. You either got it or you ain't.

But here's the good news - the rest of us can learn how to do a pretty fair imitation. And that's where a book like this comes in.

In truth, I think Spielberg would skim this book, then say - "Ah .. yeh. No, this book is nice. I can see where it would be helpful, yeh … like the section on …" - not because it actually helped him, but because he wants to help those who lack the natural instinct. In contrast, I think Edison would have taken notes - because Edison wasn't actually creative. He was simply the only man in history more innovative than George Washington Carver. This is a punchy way of introducing the

8

fact that there are only two routes to having an idea: creativity, or innovation. We'll talk about both.

The truth about creativity

We've gotten a little sloppy with the English language. We've let similar words parade around as synonyms in disguise, which confuses us anytime someone goes back to using them as distinct concepts. Do you want to eliminate the plague; maybe save 100 million lives in your lifetime? All you have to do is remember three simple things:

1. Water runs downhill
2. Hot's on the left
3. Payday is Friday

Congratulations. You just created modern plumbing; disease got neutralized and pumped far away. The most creative ideas and solutions in life tend to be so commonsensical and straight forward that we almost fail to see them as creative.

The truth about innovation

NASA spent millions trying to invent ink pens that work in zero gravity. Meanwhile, Comrade Vladmir issued pencils to the Russian Cosmonauts. That was very innovative. So was Edison's incandescent light bulb. But neither one of them was creative. You can bet your bottom dollar that we're gonna talk more about <u>that</u> later in the book.

Notice something about both of them, though.

The <u>outcome</u> - of both creativity and innovation - is usually something of pristine simplicity. But the <u>process</u> of getting there --- now that is often a different story. And *that's* the story we'll be learning, from now until page whatever it is. (I haven't finished the book yet. I simply don't know.) You see, I'm convinced that this effort is a process, not an event.

And that takes time. It also takes rules, otherwise it's just a random process - and that's neither creative nor innovative. It's just dumb luck. So here are some rules to keep us looking in the same direction.

RULE 1 - Life is not a game.

The story we're going to learn starts with an ultimate verity – Life is Not a Game. In fact, it's dead-damn serious. We die in the end, you know. And we only get to do it once. So I want to get it right, because I want my life to count for something: <u>That's</u> why I want this book to change your life. I think our actions should matter. Consequently, I don't have much patience with "gamers" who are looking for a gimmick that outsmarts the system and puts them on Easy Street. Those folks are using my air, and I don't like that.

RULE 2 - Life is complex

I know it's comforting to think otherwise, but there really isn't one single over-riding secret to life. Nor are there 3 simple rules, 4 cornerstones, or 7 magic habits that guarantee success. Obedience to the 10 commandments doesn't even guarantee you a free ticket to heaven – all the Bible promises is that obedience <u>may</u> lengthen your days upon the earth. There aren't even 12 steps that can assure us of sobriety. Life just isn't that simple.

Remember that even the one who originated the Ten Commandments had to send in his own son to straighten things out. And that didn't work out so well either, did it? It turns out that the "simple" approaches to living your life or managing people don't work consistently, because people are complex. We get tired, we lose focus, we suffer hormone cycles, we get headaches, we let up, we forget, we change our minds. So Life gets complex. It wears many shades of grey, not a simple black and white dichotomy. I am therefore tempted to suggest that you discard any book with a number in its title.

RULE 3 - Life is travel

Let's get back to a point I made earlier, all we're doing is trying to get from point A to point B. It's based on common sense. But ... how do I get Beethoven's 5th symphony from Berlin to Orlando, and preserve it (written in 1808) so that it's still fresh in 2018? I could use a bucket. But if I picked it up in 1808 I'd be dead by 2018 --- besides, the bucket leaks. So I have to make a special "sound bucket" – I'll call it a phonograph. It gets me from point A to point B.

Of course, some gaps between A and B are bigger than others. What if point A were the precise place and moment of the Big Bang, and point B is right where you're sitting, right now? How do I get one particle of matter from point A to point B when we know that space is perpetually curving and re-curving, at fluctuating speeds? I just have to make a special bucket – say the General Theory of Relativity that explains the complete space-time continuum. Point A to point B. That's all we're doing. And more than anything else, the solutions rely on common sense.

RULE 4 - Creativity is Dangerous

Most people get a kick out of innovation – but they really don't like creativity, regardless of the lip service they give it. That's because they care more about predictability and efficiency, and creativity is the enemy of both those two things. So it is seen as a danger to the organization.
- Creativity moves ahead in fits and starts & sometimes just simply wastes time and money.
- It is NOT a team sport.
- It is NOT a clear and obvious linear function.
- It is NOT predictable, AND worst of all,

- It creates change, and <u>nobody</u> likes that (they really don't).

RULE 5 – Kiss safety goodbye

Now things get scary. The ultimate irony is that creativity is most dangerous to the person who is *being* creative. Having that bright new idea can be the end of your career, or your life, depending on where you live and what the idea is.

Many people will dislike you when you're being creative, because you're the source of chaos in their lives --- and maybe even an inferiority complex to boot. As a result, they will attack and belittle you. They will marginalize and ignore you, minimize and dismiss you. They will brand you as a loose cannon, and quarantine you on the periphery as dangerous to corporate or family health. They'll accuse you of just looking for attention, and at the extreme they may take away your reputation, your job or your life. Son of a bitch!

Position does not protect you. Even the Chairman of General Motors can, and has been, summarily canned because of his ideas. The same is true all up and down the corporate ladder. So don't hide behind the fact that you may only be a middle manager. It doesn't get any easier in the corporate boardroom.

Imagine, if you will, how flabbergasted Jesus must have felt. He was the son of God, which I would argue, is a step *above* Chairman of General Motors. He made a good-will tour and shared a message that was a radical departure from the contemporary theology of rules, vendetta and judgment. Instead he offered the following good news:
- God doesn't belong to any one tribe, city or nation
- God loves you and wants you to make it
- All you have to do is say thanks
- That's it. Welcome home.

So they executed him – for instigating chaos and corrupting the morals of the community. You'll notice that the Greeks condemned Socrates for the exact same reason. Hmmm. There seems to be a universal truth in operation here: the world tends to devour change agents.

So why in the world would anyone want to be creative?

- Because there simply isn't a better feeling in the world than the incredible buzz that comes from having a new idea. It is as close to divinity as it's possible for a human to get. And we can do it everyday. It is, quite simply, the world's greatest drug.
- In addition, having an idea gets us out of the traffic jam of life. We mill around point A wondering what to do until (bam!) it hits us. "I know! Let's invent someplace to go. Let's call in point B." Voila!
- A third reason to be creative involves wealth and glory. I'd like both, but I'd settle for either one. Creativity opens the door.
- On top of all that - creativity keeps the attic lit. It stimulates the mind, and invites the soul and the heart to join in.

I'm having one of those magic moments as I sit here writing this, in a place you'll never visit, at a time that will never return. Then – poof. It's gone. But still I wear a little smile because I know that you are now sharing that moment in your own frame of time and place and I have achieved some level of immortality because you may have just picked this out of a dust bin in another century, on another planet. (I'd like to think they took this book with them. You know, the colonists.)

In short, people pursue creativity
to make a mark, to leave a legacy.

And the leader, manager or firm that understands and protects
Creatives, multiplies their impact on the world. And that
clearly gives you the upper hand in life. I'd like you to have
that hand.

And I want it to be a learned hand. There's a lot of religion,
governance, economics and science in this book. There's also
a fair amount of sociology, psychology, sex and relationships.
And cartoons as well. It is a veritable stew of Western
culture. I did that intentionally - for a very personal reason.
Too many organizations - especially in politics and religion -
are run by leaders who brag about what they *don't* know, and
I think it's time for that to end.

I actually believe you're a better leader when you know
history, theology, economics and the lot. Because, knowledge
is power. Knowledge shows you the weak points and
strengths, hopes and dreams, pasts and futures of the world
you face - and its inhabitants. And the lack of that knowledge
puts a blindfold on you while you dance through the machete
factory.

If you're culturally illiterate,
you're not just limited -
you're dangerous.

2
BUMPING INTO THE WALL
(THE DIFFERENCE BETWEEN INNOVATION & CREATIVITY)

The Swiss mastered time keeping centuries ago, with a
mechanical approach based on gear wheels and mainsprings.
They also built a wall around their minds by specializing in
the mechanical approach and ignoring all others.

On the up side, that wall focused their attention on the minute
details of craftsmanship and gave them an expertise that led to
marvelous innovations. They perfected the use of resilient,
light weight metals. They excelled in artistic design. And
they continuously developed ever more efficient production
techniques. As a result, the Swiss controlled 68% of the
world's watch market by 1968, and 80% of world profits.

However, the wall also caused them to ignore a monumental
discovery made by one of their own researchers in 1967. He
had developed a watch that was based on a completely new

idea -- that time could be traced electrically rather than mechanically. The result was the digital quartz watch. It was cheaper to make, more accurate and far more durable than mechanical watches. But the idea lay so far outside the existing wall that the Swiss manufacturers didn't even bother to patent it. However, they did take a sample digital watch to the 1968 trade show as a crowd pleasing gimmick.

This is what a fatal error looks like. It's usually very small; in this case about 30 square inches of display space. Seiko and Texas Instruments saw the new watch, grabbed the unprotected idea and the rest, as they say, is history. Ten years later the Swiss served only 10% of the watch market and their mechanical time-keeping industry had collapsed.

What Does This Tell Us?

The best thing about other people's mistakes is that <u>we</u> feel no pain. The second best thing is that we can learn something from them, if we pay attention. What does the Swiss debacle teach us?

1. **This business about the wall is important.** It affects the welfare of individuals, groups and nations. You can't walk away from something like that. If you don't master it, it will master you.

2. **Organizations don't have ideas. People do** - individuals like you and me. Consequently, this book is going to focus on the individual. It doesn't say much about the organization at all. That's a topic for another book.

3. **The difference between fantasy and creativity is action**. If you don't do anything about it, even the best idea is no more than a pipe dream. It'll just fade away into nothingness, like the smoke rings that waft skyward.

The Wall of Rationality

Most of us live within a "wall of rationality", which is a marvelous invention of civilization, made from the traditional wisdom concerning what the world is like and how we ought to approach it.

This makes for an orderly, predictable world. Very cozy. Very safe. The problem is --- the really good ideas live out beyond the wall, in the endless meadow of the mind; where revelation and wonder roam free and unfettered. Creativity is the act of severing the tether and vaulting over the wall; jumping beyond the constraints imposed by the laws of nature, work rules, competitive pressures or technological ignorance. It assumes that the old way is wrong, or at least incomplete, and leaps out into the meadow where the wild things grow.

Problems with the Wall
Life within the wall is safe and secure. In addition to being one of the wall's positive points, that is also one of its negative attributes. It lulls us into lethargy. Why would anyone want to escape from comfort?

And therein lies the difficulty. One way or another, most of us develop a liking for the current wall, which creates problems for society ... because we develop a stake in squelching creativity. The projectile-hurling first grader might just become NASA's leading scientist if we give him a star for marksmanship instead of 10 minutes in the corner. Who knows, maybe he's Orville Wright discovering the laws of aerodynamics, or Einstein having an original thought, or simply Tom Paine striking a reasoned blow for independence. Or ... maybe he's just a jerk. The problem is that we're so concerned with the sanctity of the wall, that we never bother to find out. Instead, we tend to carpet bomb the outliers.

As a result, the Wall of Rationality becomes an enormous obstacle to creativity. It patterns our behavior to such a degree that after spending years acting within the boundaries, we forget what it feels like to even **think** outside of them.

17

When we try to be creative, the best we usually do is bump along the inside of the wall looking for a cute idea that hasn't already been used. The problem is that there aren't many of those critters left. Everyone else has been grazing in the same corral for generations.

- This is a problem in business, manufacturing, automotive mechanics, and the like, since it passes the lead to our competitors.
- But it is a downright tragedy in constructing the basic tenants of the world. At that point, the Wall becomes the enemy of mankind, even though mankind huddles within its seemingly safe confines.

The wall is the last refuge of a failing entity.

I have a confession to make.

This book sat half written in a file cabinet for 15 years because I couldn't answer one simple question ---- why did I say Einstein was creative, but Edison wasn't? You and I both know that Edison was creative too. But he just didn't fit the definition I'd come up with - and I didn't know what to do about that. So I set the whole thing aside for 15 years. Then I finally figured out <u>why</u> they were both creative. They'd both been playing outside the wall of rationality. It's just that they had been dealing with different walls, in different locales:

- Einstein on the mountain top, with abstract ideas
- Edison in the trenches, with concrete ideas.

This one simple observation opened my eyes, and everything which follows is a result of this one little epiphany. Here's my brain teaser for you ----- once you step beyond the wall, where do you want to go?

- How do you want to use this tool called creativity?

- Do you want to exploit the current system in which you find yourself? Or do you want to change it?
- What drives you: the quest for wealth and glory, or the welfare of mankind?
- Are you looking for one good idea, or a whole new way to think?
- Do you need things to be concrete, or are you happy as a clam with mushy thought?
- What counts as long term for you: a month or a century?
- Is there such a thing as ultimate truth?
- Would you know it if you saw it?

Your answers to these kinds of questions will tell you where to go once you step outside the wall. And for the sake of simplicity, let's consider just two options:

1. you can work on the mountain top, or
2. you can work in the trenches.

Life on the Mountain Top is pretty heady stuff. You dine with Copernicus, Marx and Gandhi. You debate with Galileo, Cicero and Franklin. Thomas Jefferson stops by for cocktails with Mozart and his friends, Henry Ford and Michelangelo. And you, personally, spend your life looking for that next big thing that alters the course of human history … from the top down. You know … the nature of man, time, gravity, hope, truth, justice and the American Way.

Life in the trenches is a different story. You dedicate yourself to ideas that'll grab an extra 6% of market share, decrease turnover, or raise the test scores of your 8th grade class 9 points. And in the process you'll bump into things like the auto, the TV and the i-phone, things that change the way we live --- from the bottom up.

The bulk of life is lived in the trenches, not on the mountain top. But if some of us weren't up there taking on the big issues, the rest of us would soon run out of new things to do down here in the trenches. And when that happens, society implodes. Education stagnates, then ceases altogether, because – frankly – what's the point? Then the economy falters. But the ensuing mass unemployment is dwarfed by the fact that our military hasn't come up with a new weapon in 200 years so we're left fighting a short final battle with some nation (or planet) who kept growing and changing --- because they had the good sense to encourage some of their people to live on the mountain top, with their heads in the clouds – chasing the ultimate verities of life.

This book is dedicated to creativity on the mountain top. Without it, we fail as a society.

But, let's take a closer look at that. On the mountain top, the idea is the thing. Without it nothing moves. After it arrives, nothing is ever the same. Without the idea of an airplane, nobody has the foggiest notion of whether to use wings, whirly tops or just light a candle under the damn thing.

Managers tend to underestimate the value of the idea. They want to rush immediately from the drawing board to the trenches; application is the end all and be-all for them. Academics, on the other hand, tend to avoid the trenches. They simply want to bathe in the idea itself and use it to generate other ideas.

There's actually merit on both sides of the argument, but truth and beauty obviously exist somewhere in between. Since it's your turn to rule the world, you need to figure out exactly where. I can't tell you that. Well, actually, I could.

(Actually - I will. I champion the mountain top). But don't blindly accept my word as an edict from God, because that would condemn you to obsolescence. What works for me and my generation, won't work for you and yours. So here's what I'm going to do – I'm going to spend my time teaching you about the nature of ideas and the struggle to have them. By the time I'm done, you'll have the smell of them in your head. And by that point, you'll be able to set your own balance point between ideas and applications, between action and reflection, between courage and contemplation.

- So here we are – focusing on ideas.
- We might as well address the hardest point first.
- You can't just snap your fingers and conjure an idea.
- Creativity doesn't work that way.
- I am convinced that is because of the wall.

Revisiting the Wall

You cannot talk about creativity without confronting the wall. Like Moby Dick in the morning mist, the wall sits on the horizon like a silent, beckoning leviathan - calling men to their fate (perhaps, doom). It is no small thing. It is not a little waist-high lattice fence surrounding your garden. When we speak of the wall relative to creativity, we are talking about something that dwarfs the Great Wall of China, and you don't have a ladder. Perhaps the Walls of Mordor capture it better. The wall is more than simply an obstacle to vision, movement and progress. It is the thing that defines vision, movement and progress. It makes us small. And to the Creative, that is the death of hope. Ask any prisoner the central feature of his incarceration – the answer rings back -------- "the wall".

When you realize that, you realize what the Creative is doing. He is waging a lifelong war against that damned monstrosity. It is an intimate battle. The wall has personality and moral value in the eyes of the Creative. It is a thing in and of itself – an adversary with whom to wrestle.

But realize this – the Creative is <u>not</u> a rebel. In fact he is the most conservative of all God's children. Because he knows that the world is driven by structure and pure, unimpeded logic, and he has dedicated his life to discovering that true and complete structure and the logic and rationality that comprises it.

In short, every Creative is searching for the "true" Wall of Rationality. The good one. God's wall. He just knows that the current one isn't it.

> That is why a new idea,
> all by itself, is sacred.
> By its mere existence it proves that
> ultimate truth lies somewhere
> outside the current wall

So he has to get beyond the current wall, often by harming it. He sometimes does this with a heavy heart, but do it he must. He'll tear it down, blow a hole in it; install a gate, build a ramp; whatever it takes. But one way or another, he'll get beyond the current wall – the current structure that explains the world. That makes him look like a rebel – but realize that he travels in disguise. The Creative is actually the conservator of the future. And once he discovers that new wall, he will fall victim to the trap, and he will seek to protect <u>his</u> wall against every challenge from the next generation of Creatives. Today's adventurer is tomorrow's jailer. And so it goes.

How did this book get written?

I've already told you that my basic tenant is that individuals have ideas, not groups, collectives, corporations or governments. Individuals. Consequently, it seemed that biography might be the best way to learn about creativity on the mountain top. Pick those who'd breathed that rarefied air. Study their lives and see what we can learn. So I studied 33 "big picture" heroes (Aristotle, Copernicus, Isaac Newton, Napoleon, etc). It could have been 64 or 129, but I stopped at 33 because I was already seeing patterns repeated over and over again, and I've got other things going on in my life. So I invoked the rule of "good enough" and called a halt to the research.

- Is it complete? No. It doesn't pretend to be.
- Is it biased? Yep. I'm American and worked within my cultural bias.
- Did I do scientific sampling? No again. It was purely and simply a convenience sample.

So is the work invalid? Not on your life. No work is ever complete. No work is ever without bias. I'm just telling you these things so you'll have your eyes open and your minds forewarned when you read the book.

And one last tidbit --- I picked four of the people to represent the whole pack. Reporting on all 33 would have required too much information. Way too much (I stopped counting at 5,671 pages). You have things to do. So four measly lives will mold how you think, and therefore determine the development of creativity in the 21st century. I like the simplicity of that.

I'm asking you to change the world, though, so credibility is key. Some of that comes from the research itself. Some of it comes from the inherent logic and contextual consistency of the writing. And the acid test is this --- does it ring true with what you observe in your own life?

A final source of credibility is the author's life, because that is the major source of his perspective and interpretations. So let me lay it out for you. I'm a straight white male with a PhD from Northwestern and ten years experience running an organization. I've been on the faculties of some of the leading business schools in America, and I've spent the last 20 years as consigliere to America's owners. It has been my privilege to serve as father confessor, comforter, drill sergeant, strategist, consultant, advisor and confidant to the owners, CEOs and top executives of 60 businesses doing billions of dollars per year, with hundreds of employees and truck loads of challenges. I've been around the block.

Let's jump in, shall we?

3

THE PLAYERS
(THE INVENTION PROCESS)

To illustrate how this war against the wall plays out, we're going to host a little party – one with a very short guest list.

- Albert Einstein brings greetings from the world of science.
- Martin Luther will be the delegate from religion
- Ben Franklin stands in for the governments of the world.
- Adam Smith, the most revolutionary of them all, represents the everyday commerce of life.

They stand as surrogates for the handful of folks who changed the world. Note, however, that none of them was a president, king or general. As it turns out, leadership - especially vision-based leadership - does not depend on station, title or prestige.

In fact, one was an effete tutor, one a passive-aggressive whiner, one an inveterate tinkerer and one a very angry monk. And all they did was turn the world on its ear. Imagine, then, what *you* can do.

- Luther showed us that every man can stand toe to toe with God Almighty, know His heart and discover His will - because God is a benevolent god, not a fire breathing dragon.
- Franklin showed us that every man can stand toe to toe with a king, and more importantly, that man does not even need a king.
- Adam Smith showed us that every man can be the equal of his neighbor, oddly enough, by serving his neighbor.
- And Einstein showed us that every man is hurtling through the cosmos on a beam of light, past the Vulcans into the great abyss.

Their stories will unlock the core of vision-based leadership.

A little background

The world has been this way before. That's the scary part of the story. For millions of years man lived a brutish existence, fighting with the elements and each other for every morsel. Then we finally learned to live in small groups and city-states began to dot the landscape. Progress was slow and painfully convoluted, mostly because man had a need to periodically carouse, strong-arm each other's women and engage in fits of carnage; all of which carried us back a few steps toward grunting in caves, each time it happened.

Then the gods showed up. They traveled as a family (well, as a soap opera family - where your Mom, sister and cousin were all the same person) and they ran the world by whim. They were a screwed up family of miscreants, egotists and narcissists; and they used man as a pawn in their jealous little parlor games. Gods, it turns out, were the lowest form of life, except for their otherworldly power. So man had to suck up to them to postpone his own inevitable humiliation and demise. Needless to say, fear was a dominant theme of the day, and man earned his survival by placating these morons with his own exemplary behavior. Heathens were initially stunned by the absurdity of this goody-two-shoes approach to life, until they came to understand its obvious truth and accuracy. It was the only explanation that fit reality. What else could possibly account for the arbitrary and capricious destruction of fire and flood, earthquake and famine except for the petulance of a spoiled child with supernatural powers. So the heathen became a believer, and started to fit into society.

It was also the only thing that seemed to put a curb on man's baser instincts. I scoff at Freud's theory that man invented God. How absurd. Clearly divinity was the center of the natural order of the universe. It brought order. It brought peace. It brought predictability. But it was a tad bit confining, when it came to thinking.

Then the planets aligned, or some such magic settled on the earth, and we got a 3-fer (3 for the price of one) in Socrates, Plato and Aristotle. One taught the next, who taught the next who let the genie out of the bottle and changed the course of history.

Socrates entered this world of arbitrary divines like a thunderclap. Perhaps, he stated, the world is a logically constructed place, with its own rules and regulations --- not the whim-driven parlor of infantile petulants. If so, perhaps we can reason our way to discovering how the world actually works, and wean ourselves from these silly gods.
Socrates introduced the logical stream – a process by which one question leads to another, then another, then another – peeling the onion until we discover the underlying cause and reason of things. And that underlying cause, it turns out, is

27

never a god. So the Greeks killed him; for corrupting the young with sacrilege and scaring the hell out of the city council. Little did they know. That was small potatoes.

Like Osama bin Ladin, Socrates true subversive punch came from the fact that he'd educated a generation of Greek boys before the authorities got to him. Plato was one of them, and he picked up Socrates' mantel and became the next great teacher, telling his students that the logical stream (the Socratic Method) should be applied to the "big picture" issues – the nature of man, why he interacts, the essence of governance and why we do it, the concept of a republic. He was the world's first out-and-out intellectual egghead, going on about "chair-ness" and essence, and shadows versus reality.

Now Plato's best student was Aristotle, but he went the opposite way. He said we were best served to use Socrates' logical stream down in the trenches, on the mundane little things of life. Instead of discourses on the concept of sitting, and the essence of chair-ness, Aristotle focused first on categorizing the world:
- sitting is but one of the ways we rest, let us list the others;
- there are numerous things on which we could rest, let us list and define them;
- chairs can have infinite variety, let's enumerate what we see;
- then let's clump them into groups according to similarities;
- then let's measure them and find out what they're made of.

The second thing he did was establish a system for explaining how these things acted on one another. He came up with a system of reason, a causal chain – prime causes, secondary causes, responsive causes, external and internal causes etc. And the cause always had to be something _observable by the_ *senses.* In other words, you weren't allowed to invoke the smoke and mirrors of "god-ness".

That's Socrates main point – in another guise. But instead of killing Aristotle, the authorities gave him a prince to educate. You see, by then, the eggheads were everywhere. There were just too damn many of them. Plus, they made too much sense to kill. So you did the next best thing. You used them to educate kings. Phillip of Macedonia hired Aristotle to teach his son – who turned out to be Alexander the Great – the kid who conquered the entire known world by age 32, using the science of Aristotle and Archimedes, the philosophy of Plato and the dedication to reason from Socrates.

The Roman's took over from the Greeks, in one of the gentlest transitions of empire on record – to the point where the Romans kept the Greeks' religion, philosophy and culture, simply adding their own genius for engineering, transportation and commerce. And the army. Yup. Rome did have an army. For five hundred years, the world prospered. There was a unified "world" government. Communication and commerce moved with lightening speed. There was surplus and leisure. Arts flourished. Education soared.

Then man got stupid

The empire collapsed, the libraries got burned. The intelligentsia was executed. The Taliban had arrived. The eggheads were eliminated and life went back to the way God intended it – ruled by manly men - brutish, ignorant thugs - all driven by an angry God who punished us at His whim. And if Hell is worse than this – imagine how bad that must be. We call the next 800 years the Dark Ages. All progress ceased. Except in the Catholic church, which used – some say supported - the Dark Ages as an avenue to greatness.

- Literacy disappeared, except in the church.
- Education disappeared, except in the church.

- Likewise art and philosophy, except in the church.

And the church became the shadow government throughout
the western world – using ignorance, and the fear of Hell as its
club. Petulance had returned to divinity, and the church was
its muscle ... the grand enforcer.

> **Now** we're ready to meet our guests,
> and see what a Wall of Rationality can truly be.

4

COMING TO GRIPS WITH THE WALL

Luther and the Pope's Wall

Luther grew up within the supreme fortress of all time – the Roman Catholic Church of the 15th century. Talk about a Wall of Rationality that defined and directed behavior… this was it. The world was ruled by an angry god, and each of us was doomed to eternal perdition by our own innate sinfulness. Eternal perdition, remember, was a living nightmare of physical torture and emotional terror that went on forever.

And the church was the only thing that could save your hind end, because God had given the keys to heaven, and the secret knowledge about how heaven and earth worked to the first Pope - St. Peter, himself. Those secrets had been passed from one Pope to the next and the current Pope would share just enough of this magic with you to keep you out of Hell, via a cannibalistic ritual called communion. You would be given a tiny piece of flesh from the body of Christ and a few drops of his blood. And in consuming them, God would forgive you --- for a while. Then you'd have to eat more Jesus next week.

Christ had given communion to Peter. He'd given it to the next pope and eventually a pope gave communion to the cardinals, who'd given it to the bishops, who'd given it to the local priests. So the secrets, and the power of the body and blood had come down to you in a direct unbroken line from the hand of God himself. But if you irritated the local priest, he would cut you off. No communion for you. No communion, no salvation. You were Hell-bound with no recourse whatsoever.

Not surprisingly, the church was a powerful force in the secular world; determining who would be king, who could have land, who would be slave or free. When someone holds your eternal pain or pleasure in their hands, you tend to cave in to whatever they demand. Including what to think.

So 15th century Europe "knew" the stars, moon and sun rotated around the earth. Disease and deformity were signs of the victim's sin and guilt. Earthquakes, hurricanes and forest fires were personally triggered by God to kill people that displeased him. Loaning money was a sin. Lusting after a woman was a sin. Being human was a sin. Have a good day.

God was omniscient (all knowing), omnipotent (all powerful), omnipresent (everywhere at once), and transcendent (hovering above the fray). And as his personal delegate to this world, so was the church. Amen, and again I say Amen.

Protecting the wall

One last thing about this wall: they put you to death if you tried to climb it. Their favorite method was immolation – burning someone at the stake - but they were open to other methods as well. They even practiced "humane" exits such as the quick and painless beheading. This was one serious mother-lovin' wall of rationality, and protecting it was such an important task that the Vatican instituted a special department, run by its most favored cardinal – specifically dedicated to burning anyone who even claimed that something worthwhile lived on the other side of the wall.

That department was called the Holy Office of the Inquisition, and each cardinal who ran it was known as the Grand Inquisitor. Not surprisingly, each cardinal who ran it had the inside track on becoming the next Pope.

In the 1490s, the Grand Inquisitor was especially favored by King Ferdinand and Queen Isabella – who had just recently managed to kick the last Muslim Army out of Spain. They were using the church to light up the night sky with any Muslim or Jew who did not convert, and the sky was very bright. If the names sound familiar, it's because they are the same Ferdinand and Isabella who financed Columbus' voyage of discovery. Isn't history amazing?

Pretend this is a footnote.
But don't read it if you're squeamish ... (or Catholic)

Eventually, the world grew weary of the church's habit of burning heretics, so in the 1800s the church shifted to burning books instead. But when Hitler started to copy that tactic they decided that yet another image change was in order. So they changed the Inquisition's name to the Congregation for the Doctrine of the Faith. And the Grand

---

Inquisitor's title was softened to "Prefect", but it's mission remained the same and the sanctions it could use were (and are) left undefined in the Vatican's constitution.

And that brings us to an interesting little historical footnote. Pope Benedict XVI became pope in 2005. Go ahead, ask me what he'd been just before then. Go ahead. I dare you. Yep. He'd spent the prior 24 years as the Grand Inquisitor. And here's a cute little footnote to the footnote – The Grand Inquisitor is also the officer in charge of protecting parishioners from sexual abuse by the clergy. Apparently he let some things slide if you touted the party line. Does any of this make you feel just a little creepy? Especially in light of Benedict's decree in July of 2007 that the Catholic faith is the only way to avoid the fires of Hell. It feels like a giant step back in history.

And then Pope Benedict suddenly "retired". The first one in history to do so. A pope doesn't retire, ladies and gentlemen. He dies --- in office, with his boots on, as the lordly shepherd of an enormous world-wide congregation. One suspects that Benedict was retired by the College of Cardinals, in a quiet palace coup. No substantive reason was ever given. He just disappeared.

But enough of current events. Let's get back to Columbus.

Christopher Columbus

Chris isn't a guest at our little soirée. But if it hadn't been for him, none of the rest of the story would have happened. So we're going to take a moment to consider him. Driven purely by the dream of wealth and glory, Columbus hit land in 1492. By about 1497 folks started to realize that it wasn't actually the coast of China. It was, instead, an entire continent that no one had known existed. No one. Not even the Pope. Yikes!

Religion for the Lost Boys

If the church was really omniscient the Pope and clergy - and scriptures - should have known that a continent that size was floating around out there. And if they'd known it they surely would have told us, long ago. So is the church really omniscient? And if not, what else might not be true? Hmmm. One knows for a fact that European teenagers latched onto these questions the same way my son's generation grabbed hold of President Clinton's redefinition of sex (it ain't sex unless its sex [you know, penetration]). Columbus was the heavy metal star of his day - like KISS, creating a lost generation of kids who gleefully believed in nothing.

We know this because a generation later, in 1517 Luther stepped onto the world stage with his "nailing the theses to the door" stunt --- and the world slipped easily into revolution --- one that spread across all of Europe. They'd let the church broil every critic who'd come before. It wasn't Luther that exploded onto the stage. It was Columbus' lost generation.

Do the math. A 15 year old in 1497 was the same as a 15 year old today. He was feeling his oats, chomping on the bit and endlessly frustrated at living under the old man's thumb. He was dying to find something at which he was smarter and better, anxious to change something big to leave his own mark in the world. And Columbus just proved that every authority figure in life was ignorant, not just wrong. The teenagers were gleeful at watching the pompous get popped – but they woke up the next morning and realized they had nothing to believe in.

For almost 2 decades they had nothing to believe in. By 1517 that 15 year old boy had become a 35 year old man. He was a pillar of the community, served in the militia, manned the buckets when fire struck, supported a wife and kids – and served as the truth-giver to the next generation. And he still had nothing to believe in. He knew the old tried and true stuff was no longer guaranteed. He just didn't know what to replace it with. Luther provided an answer.

Franklin and the King's Wall

In comparison, <u>Ben Franklin</u> had it easy. He didn't have to fight God or the Pope. All he had to do was take on the King. Well, actually – he had to take on the concept of monarchy in general.

Since the time of the first Pharaoh, the world had been ruled by kings. There was no other way to do it, really. At least none other had succeeded for more than a moment. In addition to that, King David, in the Old Testament, made up a policy, all on his own, which he claimed came from God.

It was called **the Divine Right of Kings:** God chooses a king and, therefore, everyone must obey him and no one is allowed to kill him or dethrone him. It was a nifty bit of self-serving statecraft that affected the rest of world history.

- One extension of the divine right was the presumption of wisdom. Since the king is God's anointed, he must know more than me.
- Another extension was the vassal obligation. Since the king is God's anointed, I serve the king – as I would serve my God.
- Another extension was the sacrilege of change. It is sacrilege, and not just treason, to contemplate changing

the natural order (the upstairs/downstairs world) that God has established.

- Consequently, the average man has no rights, and only those privileges temporarily granted by the wise king, which could be withdrawn if foolishly used.
- Finally, since everything ultimately belongs to God, and since the king is God's anointed agent, everything ultimately belongs to the king. Therefore, all power flows downhill, from the king.

Being a king was a pretty sweet gig. And the logistics of time and space conspired to keep it that way. Check out a map. Europe is surprisingly small and compact. It's pretty easy to be omnipresent, omniscient and omnipotent when everything is within 2 hours of everything else. But right around 1480, the sciences of shipbuilding and navigation suddenly popped a big one. Man finally figured out longitude, so they could calculate how far east and west they'd traveled, which is crucial if your only option is sailing west from Europe. This, plus Columbus' courage, expanded the world by a factor of ten.

The old monarchy model was simply incapable of controlling such a vastly enlarged universe. It now took about 90 days for the king to ask his subjects in the new world for a cup of tea, as opposed to the 5 minutes it took within the confines of his original kingdom. And while it only required an hour to catch and punish someone who refused his wishes in Europe – it took a minimum of 6 months and enormous expense to do the same if one of the colonists demurred. And more often than not enforcement was impossible because the transgressor simply faded into the endless wilderness.

The divine right of kings lost its divinity due to technology. The wall of rationality that surrounded monarchy was ready to be crested and not just by the American colonies. In 1776 Ben Franklin showed up with his own ladder. He was the ghost writer of the Declaration of Independence, helping young Thomas Jefferson craft the document read 'round the world. He was the one man who so charmed the French that they decided to forget the war we'd just fought against them (The French and India War) and back our revolution against the British - that had no chance of victory - thereby guaranteeing it's success. Franklin was also the glue that held together the constitutional convention, which actually created the United States of America, 11 years later. He was a force of nature, and world history has trod a different path because he lived.

Smith and the Ego Wall

At the exact same time, 1776, Adam Smith was at war with something far more amorphous than a king a pope or a god. He was at war with society in general, and its norms.

The divine right of kings had spawned an extension: whereas everything ultimately belongs to God, and whereas the King is God's agent here on earth …

therefore … everything belongs to the king. So he has the right to take it back any time he wants. In other words, the king had the right to confiscate whatever he wanted, whenever he wanted.

The divine right of kings also spawned yet another extension - that the king's wealth was a sign of God's favor. This was very interesting, since poverty was the sign of God's favor for everyone else. Anyway, human nature being what it is, kings tended to be a bit competitive. Every king wanted to be the richest one, since that meant God loved him most. It also meant more women, but let's stick to the theological veneer. The question became - how do you measure "rich"?

Obviously, by the gap between the king and his own peasants. If they lived in small tents and the king just lived in a big one, then the king wasn't all that rich, so God didn't really love him.   And if God didn't favor you as a king – you were dead meat. The other kings wouldn't respect you and they'd start to attack; and in pretty short order you'd no longer be a king. In fact, in pretty short order you'd be dead.

- So kings built stone houses, then manor estates, then castles.
- But they kept their peasants in little more than small tents.
- And the gap between peasant and king grew.
- And the king looked and lo – he was rich.
- But his country stayed poor as a church mouse. In fact, Europe was infested by around 100 kingdoms; each with about 1 acre of opulence (a couple of woven tapestries and a china plate) and miles of abject poverty and filth.

Another extension of the divine right of kings was that it was a sin to focus on wealth if you weren't a king. The church conspired with the kings to make sure the gap between rich and poor remained unchallenged because the king kept the church in fish and chips. It was a classic duopolistic system. I scratch your back, you scratch mine – and we screw everyone else. The church played its role in this little drama via two theological interpretations.

First – the church declared that poverty was the mark of righteousness, in keeping with the Apostle Paul's admonition – "Lay not up for yourself treasures on earth where moth and rust doth corrupt, but lay up for yourself treasures in heaven, for where your treasure is, there will your heart be also." Therefore, any peasant who tried to amass wealth was, get this, "uppity" in that he was trying to move up the social ladder. And the church, and the king's court dealt harshly with him. That, combined with the outright confiscation of crops, property, animals and children by the king made sure no <u>individual</u> peasant could challenge the king. No wonder Robin Hood was popular.

Second – the church outlawed usury – the practice of loaning money at interest. Without it, it was impossible to amass the kind of capital folks needed in order to create group ventures like collective farms or factories and you know – start an industrial revolution. Cottage industry was held up as the praiseworthy mark of a righteous life, whereby every family took care of its own needs, made its own nails and pins and grew its own food. Just the thought of a factory was sinful. That way, the peasants – <u>as a group</u> – couldn't challenge the king's wealth either.

Then, having made their lives untenable, the king and the church worked mightily to prevent the inevitable rebellion by convincing the peasants that this is what their parents and forebears had wanted and ordained.
- It was not just the will of God.
- It was not just the divine right of kings.
- It was something engrained in the DNA.

Some men were created, by God, to rule. The rest were created to lick his floor clean, and feel damned lucky to have the snack. Service, not happiness, was the repeated mantra. Man lives to serve, lives to serve, lives to serve. Duty, honor, country. It wasn't the US Marines that invented that phrase. Any thought of one's own comfort and ease was therefore downright unnatural and caused one's own family to be aghast.

It is hard for us in 21st century America to comprehend this upstairs/downstairs mentality or the fact that people would buy into it. But it was the backbone of European culture until World War II, and still thrives in India's caste system and elsewhere.

People readily believe the worst, or least, about themselves.

* * * * *

It is believing the *best* that requires heroic efforts and monumental proofs.

The final extension of The Divine Right was the law of unintended results. The King and his nobles had labored mightily to create an idyllic world. They used their wisdom on behalf of the peasants and thereby saved them from the anguish of making decisions for themselves. All the peasant had to do was be obedient, cheerful and loyal. But instead, much to the king's surprise, they were insolent, lazy and treasonous. So the king and his nobles had commissioned a class of thinkers for a thousand years. They were known as the moral philosophers, and their charge was to remake the beast. In short, their task was to teach the peasants to rise above the brutish, ignorant thuggery into which the king, himself, had dragged them. Interesting challenge, that.

- Adam Smith, like every other man of the upper crust in Great Britain, followed the grand experiment (the American colonies) with extreme interest.
- He, like others, could see the divine right of kings unraveling for 50 years before the revolution ignited.
- He, like others, could see the king's power slipping away.
- And he like others, actually wanted to preserve the monarchy and much of the culture that enabled it to survive – not because he loved the idea of kings, but

because he feared the chaos that not having a king would bring.

 So in 1776, Adam Smith published <u>The Wealth of Nations</u>, a handbook on how a king could grow his wealth and power by manipulating *the economy*. Smith's goal was to provide new rules for running a far-flung empire and it was to serve as a companion piece to T<u>he Prince,</u> Machiavelli's handbook on how a king could grow his wealth and power by manipulating *politics*.

His effort got pre-empted by the Revolutionary War, which he didn't realize at the time. In fact, the 2nd and 3rd editions of his book, published prior to the end of the war referred to it in the past tense as the "recent difficulties in the colonies". Regardless, his book has had an even larger impact on the world than our Declaration of Independence. He created the engine for the merchant class, in every country and economic system, and rewrote the cultural norms that drive us to this day. He also provided the visible fist (economic might) that creates and protects individual rights. In truth, he was a moral philosopher, not an economist.

Einstein and Newton's Wall

Sir Isaac Newton single-handedly drove the final nails into the coffin of mysticism and ushered the western world firmly into the scientific age by writing down 4 simple laws back in 1687 that explained how most of the world worked in simple mechanical terms.

1. The universal law of gravitation – every object is attracted to every other object, by a force pointing along the line attaching the two; proportional to their masses and inversely proportional to the distance between them.

2. The 1st law of motion - An object in motion will remain in motion unless acted upon by a net force, an object at rest will remain at rest unless acted upon by a net force

3. The 2nd law of motion - Force equals mass multiplied by acceleration

4. The 3rd law of motion - To every action there is an equal and opposite reaction

That was it. But those 4 little laws explained damn near all of nature and thereby took away the church's mysticism – its strongest weapon in the battle against secularism and the peasantry.

Newton destroyed the mysteries of the church, by showing that things occurred due to immutable laws of nature – which operated independent of moody deities. It didn't matter whether you sucked up to the priest or not – water would still run down hill. Bang.

From that point on, Newton was elevated to the role of secular messiah and Newtonian physics and the empirical "Scientific Method" was the new wall of rationality that ruled Europe. The age of empiricism had arrived. You couldn't even say "Good day" without having to define your terms and prove your hypothesis. How fun. At least it was better than the prior ritual response to "Good day" --- which was, "Only if god does not, this day, chose to drop us into the fiery abyss". Newton became an icon in his own lifetime; more popular than kings. He was the matinee idol of his day. And in the Scientific Method ruled the roost:

Theory → Hypothesis → Test (rinse & repeat)

Science and technology leapt ahead, culminating in the Industrial Revolution , which altered the face, and history, of planet earth.

Two centuries later, however, people started noticing little chinks in Newton's wall. Nothing big. It was just that as measuring technology improved, they started to notice that most of the predictions that grew out of his 4 laws were just a little bit off. Infinitesimal really. But noticeable. Then in 1905, Einstein scaled the wall built by Europe's secular messiah, bending the Scientific Method into a pretzel.

We'll come back to that a little later. But first, let's consider what happens anytime you try to go beyond the reining wall of rationality.

❧

5

PROTECTING THE WALL
(GAMESMANSHIP 101)

Exactly which part of Christ am I having for communion today? And how did you keep it refrigerated for 1,500 years without an Amana or Sub-Zero freezer in the cathedral? If God is the creator of all things, and if nothing which God created is sinful, and if God made sex so pleasurable that some of us want to do it all the time – how then can you say it is a sin? And, by the way, did anyone ever notice that God never says "Let there be marriage, and here's how it should work"?

These points seem screamingly sacrilegious until we realize that they are the kind of questions that were asked by Luther and a host of scholars (well – a small group of scholars) for a millennium before Luther. By creating a wall of rationality based on edict, the Catholic Church also created an incredible amount of inconsistency and contradiction which they couldn't explain away. So, in frustration, they invented transubstantiation and the infallibility of the Pope, and several other mystic doctrines - all in a classic parental retort ---
"*BECAUSE I SAID SO!*"

> Not surprisingly, that approach destroyed the dignity of the individual and created *Worm Theology* - ie - man was a worthless worm who - except for the begrudging indulgence of an angry god - would burn for all time in an unrelenting, and otherwise quite unpleasant hell. And the clergy were the only thing that stood between the worm and the coming nightmare. So the worm kowtowed before the clergy, who were the sole arbiters of who got to take communion - which was seen as the get out of jail free card. It was like having your spiritual cell phone confiscated. No communion - no communication with God. Ergo - excommunication. Think about what you're willing to do to get your cell phone back. That pales in comparison to the games played by the clergy in Luther's day.

But back to our main story … people (in and out of the power elite) play an inordinate number of head games in a vain attempt to prop up the existing wall of rationality. And the head games increase just prior to the final collapse, because fear overwhelms the last vestige of common sense.

The one that triggered Luther's Reformation was the authority of the Pope. The Pope offered a clearance sale on salvation in an effort to shore up his self-proclaimed control of the mysteries of the universe. You no longer had to do confession

46

or penance. You no longer had to make a pilgrimage to Rome. You no longer had to DO anything to save your immortal soul. Now all you had to do was fork over a little money and voila! The Pope himself would forgive your sins (a job previously held by God). It was called an indulgence. How painless. How benign. How kind and loving of both the almighty and the Pope. And only the Catholic church had the license to make this special offer – so come on down, Sunday, Funday, at International Deutsche Dragstrip.

It literally became a carnival as the Pope sent out a special troupe of priests to hawk his wares at every cathedral, church and village bazaar – complete with band and banners. It was a downright weird program, even to the died-in-the-wool loyalists in the Vatican. But the Pope did it for two reasons that were near and dear to their hearts.

1. From a theological standpoint - he wanted to reinforce the church's role as the sole arbiter of the soul's welfare in the face of constant challenges from all sides.
2. From an administrative standpoint - he'd set out to build the world's largest and grandest building, as an awe-inspiring rallying point for the faithful. But the St. Peter's Basilica project was so large that it needed a massive fund raising campaign, because - ironically - the church had outlawed banking. Ouch!

So the Pope decided to kill two birds with one stone. It turns out that the reformation was in large measure about real estate development. And you thought Donald Trump was crass.

The divine right of kings, and all that supported it, was such an engrained wall of rationality, that even the kingpins of the American Revolution did everything they could to preserve it, even at the height of their insubordination. For most of their debate they blamed their grievances on the British Parliament, not the King and were quite pointed in their formal

47

correspondence to honor the divine right while arguing against crown policy. And after a day of furiously planning an insurrection they would repair to a local pub and spend the evening drinking toast after somber toast to his gracious Britannic majesty – King George.

Perhaps the most glaring example of the games we play in support of the old order is the plethora of stunts pulled by the protectors of **Newtonian physics**. They had championed the scientific method back when Isaac first wrote his laws, in 1687.

- Form a hypothesis (or theory) about how something works
- Predict what results you will see if it's true
- Run an experiment to see if it's true
- Collect hard data
- Count it true and accurate
- If the data is a surprise, admit you were wrong
- Start again with a new hypothesis.

But technology improved and man moved from traveling by carriage at a 6 mph pace to traveling by train at a 50 mph pace. Telegraph and telephone cables crisscrossed the globe and communication that previously took weeks or months became instantaneous. Electricity had brought the wonders of daylight into the darkest night and the Circadian rhythm of night and day were forever altered. By 1900 mankind could float in air, and believed they would be able to fly like the birds in the very near future. Balloons were a mainstay in the sky and there were rampant rumors that fast flight based on wings was about to make an appearance.

Man no longer kept his eyes on the ground. Every thinking man knew that the future lay out there in the sky, traveling who knew how far, in who knew how little time. Jules

Verne's stories about trips to the moon and under the vast oceans made it sound like news reports rather than science fiction. Time and space had once again fluctuated . The physical world effectively shrunk. But the mental world expanded enormously. And in pursuing that bigger, quicker world, engineers started to run into all sorts of problems with Newton's Theories.

Their predictions were <u>always</u> off. Not by much. But always. Any time you looked further than the mechanics of your local environment (ie, your village, town or city) Newton was just a little bit wrong. So the entire scientific community conspired to deny that simple fact. They wantonly violated the very scientific method they had originally championed.

- They invented the concept of environmental measurement bias based on everything from metal stress and optical illusions to laziness and nefarious motives, and challenged any contradictory data as erroneous.
- When that failed they invented numbers, such as "Avogardo's number" to arbitrarily explain things that Newton's theory itself couldn't explain, as though gravitational pull was racing around the universe, chased by a little guy named Avogardo driving a racy little number. Even Max Plank the reigning theoretical physicist of the day joined the game, coming up with his own arbitrary contribution (Planck's Constant).
- When that failed, they just started to make stuff up. Like the "ether": an ill-defined, immeasurable, invisible cloud type thing that filled in the gaps of Newtonian based hypotheses.
- And when Newton's theory failed to correctly predict the orbit of Mercury, they outdid even Gene Roddenberry – the guy who invented Star Trek. The scientific community sagely nodded in acquiescence to the invention of an invisible planet named Vulcan (hello, Mr. Spock) that somehow managed to avoid all detection, yet exerted just enough gravitational pull on Mercury (and

Mercury alone, oddly enough) to fix Newton's predictions.

The stories go on and on to the point where absurdity becomes the norm. And from all this we can derive a simple moral lesson.

The unknown, out beyond our current wall of rationality, is so terrifying that even our most learned men have trouble granting themselves the freedom to contemplate it.

And that is what turns a fortress into a prison. This wouldn't be quite so important if it weren't for one little fact. The internet has caused time and space to double back on themselves yet again.

- Space has not shrunk, nor has it expanded. It has simply ceased to exist. We have, in essence created an intellectual black hole, compressing an enormous amount of meaning and activity into a minute space.

- Time has gone beyond instantaneous, to simultaneous. In addition, it has gone from broadcast (one talking to millions) to interactive (billions talking to billions – all at once). We have created a new tower of Babel. Except it's not a tower. It's the "ether" of Babel. Don't you love the irony?

We have not seen a technological and therefore cultural change of this magnitude since Columbus.

- Governments, as we know them, are not long for this world. A loosely knit terrorist enemy will demand a loosely knit governmental or quasi-governmental entity to battle it. Non-American American prisons and nonaccountable mercenary troops are just the start. Drones allow teenagers to make bombing runs on targets half a world away, without any personal risk whatever.

- Commerce, as we have known it, has already started the obvious part of its transformation. It is re-fragmenting into smaller, decentralized enterprises – held together by ad hoc collaboration rather than formalized organizational governance.
- Relationships and courtship, as we have known them, are shifting into the digital ether, and away from the intimacy of face to face encounter..
- Truth has become a customizable commodity, as the editorial power of a centralized media and educational establishment gives way to the chaos of competing propaganda machines.
- The concept of family has already changed. Children now grow up with 3, 4 or 5 parents depending on the fidelity of their sire and mare. Eight grandparents has now become the norm; as well as a mixed bag of full blood, ½ and step siblings, who come and go in fluid alliances.

Whether or not you feel it, our walls of rationality are teetering and we need a few brave souls to tromp into the great beyond.

Moral decay is not what's changing the world. Technology is. If we realize that, maybe it will be less frightening.

The second moral lesson here is that every Wall of Rationality creates unintended effects. That usually occurs when we start

51

to play the games that support a crumbling wall. And the truly sad part of this is that every new wall of rationality was built, in part, to free man from the absurdities of the old wall. Each new wall therefore serves as the bow of a ship of discovery and adventure, and as a shelter from chaos. It allows us to play and work in the meadow on the other side, yet return each night to the warmth of its protection. Then the first chinks appear and it quickly ceases to be a ship of discovery. The sole mission becomes the prevention of chaos. And the more it concentrates on that, the more it forces its chinks to grow into fissures. And so it goes. Some of those unintended results are treated briefly below.

Either-or Thinking

Every new movement is full of exuberant piss and vinegar. It walks in like a swashbuckler and demands allegiance, "He who is not for me, is against me. You must be hot or cold. If you are lukewarm I will spew you out." Braggadocio is one thing at the front end of a movement - but it becomes a different thing entirely at the other end of the spectrum, when that old wall of rationality is on its way out. By then it has been part and parcel of "the establishment" for quite some time and has the full power of church, academia and/or the state behind it. So in its last throes of self-defense it sets about defrocking, disbarring, excommunicating and/or executing the new kids. Either way, you're fighting over absolutes. As a result, society loses a lot of talent – and misses the third way.

Is light a particle or a wave? Newton wasn't sure, but guessed it was a particle – and that became gospel. For the next 200 years science fought over particle or wave. Then Einstein showed up and said "you're both wrong – it's a quanta – a packet of energy that behaves like both a particle and a wave. Then Zip! The world of energy (not just light) opened up as never before. Impressive – but we lost 200 years waiting for someone with the courage to state the obvious.

52

In 2001, terrorists attacked the United States and George Bush II told us we needed to give up a chunk of our freedom so that he could make us safe. He gave us the Patriot Act, which was about the scariest law in America since the Sedition Act of 200 years prior. Bush was telling us that life is an either-or proposition. You can have safety or you can have freedom. You can't have both. Interestingly, that was the same either-or that Ben Franklin confronted back in 1776. But he took a little different tack. He said the man (or nation) who is willing to trade his liberty for a bit of safety is deserving of neither. But he went on to say that everything else was negotiable. It was a third way.

The either-or mode of thought is pleasing in the short run. It simplifies the world and brings structure to the uncertainty and chaos. It also contains an implicit threat of muscle to back it up, which always feeds the testosterone. It's either my way – or the highway. It's either my way – or you get the shock and awe treatment (the internationally televised bombing of a defenseless Baghdad.) Very forceful in the short run, but it creates one hell of a mess in the long run.

The either-or mindset also hampers us with blinders. We forget that there are more than two ways to skin a cat. So we stop looking. And the day you stop looking is the day that progress stops dead in its tracks. So remember – there is always a third way.

Dining on the Sacred Cow
Every wall of rationality is built on a foundation – the unchallengeable absolutes that give rise to the individual bricks that make up the wall.
- The world is flat, so don't swim too far from shore. Likewise drifting too far from traditional wisdom in any field is equally dangerous. So don't get too creative.
- Those chosen by the Lord (ie -kings) have secret knowledge. So do not question them. Likewise, anyone

who is put over you (parent, teacher, boss, whatever) also serves at the behest of God. So never question authority of any kind – ie – don't go thinking for yourself.

- Time is an absolute. It has a set duration. It moves at a standard pace. The same is true of space. It has substance and dimension. It is concrete. I can measure them both, repeatedly, and I will get the same answer each and every time. They are set and immutable. Likewise, there are moral absolutes as well, like sin and righteousness, heaven and hell, and right and wrong. So we see that life is simple. It is black or white.

- And finally – just remember that the one constant in the universe is the speed of light. It is a constant speed and it is the fastest speed in the universe. Therefore, everything in the universe can be understood relative to the speed of light.

The problem, of course, is that living on sacred cow causes one to stop thinking. There's no need – because everything is obvious. So we forget to sail into the foreboding sea, and never know that an enormous continent even exists. We forget to challenge authority and consequently miss ever having an original thought, because we will never peek over the wall. We stare at our watch and never discover that time is relative and that space actually bends. And lest we get too smug – realize that there's also a problem with Einstein's speed of light. There is at least one thing faster. Gravity is instantaneous. Hmmm.

The methodology of thought
Here's a surprising little tidbit. Einstein never won the Nobel Prize for the Theory of Relativity --- in part because it was "too Jewish". Now what in the hell does that mean? It means he didn't think about it right. He didn't talk about it right and he didn't end up with the right conclusion. It was too, you know … Jewish. The judgment was clearly influenced by the

anti-Semitism of the day, but the fact of the matter is, they were absolutely correct. It really was very Jewish.

The ancient Jews had a culture that revolved around a concept called Nephishism – the belief that everything synthesizes and integrates with everything else in an ongoing stew of life. When the Bible tells us that Abraham knew Sarah, it's not trying to avoid the word "sex" – the Jews were a pretty earthy lot and felt no discomfort with the most graphic references. What they meant was that coitus (boinking in modern vernacular) was as much a mental joining as a physical joining. It was also, simultaneously spiritual, emotional, rational, functional and religious (hence the "Oh my god! Oh my god!" mantra still repeated today). So the only way to know if a man was righteous or not was to look at his motivations. That's where situational ethics came from – the ancient Jews deciding if one's dalliance was acceptable behavior or not. And that's the source of ethics. Hence, Judaism's official description is that it is "ethical monotheism". It shows up all over the Old Testament.

The New Testament, however, was written by an entirely different group of folks. It was written for and by Greeks – Chief among them was the Apostle Paul. These guys were very different than the ancient Jews. They were educated in the Hellenistic culture that grew out of Socrates, Plato and Aristotle. And that meant they were Gnostic, rather than Nephish.

Gnosticism stated that the various aspects of man did NOT synthesize and integrate with each other. In fact, Gnosticism went a step further and said, not only were they eternally separate – they were also mutually exclusive. You could not be both rational and emotional. You had to be one or the other. Likewise, you couldn't be sexual and spiritual at the same time. You had to be one or the other. And on down the line it went. So if you were going to be stuck in a box, but you still had the burden of being a moral man – you had to figure out which aspect beat which on the moral scoreboard. That's how western culture came up with it's pecking order. Paul was big on the Spirit versus Flesh. That's where his quote "Lay not us treasures on earth ..." came from. Paul was a Gnostic. Big Time. And since he is the single biggest contributor to the New Testament – western culture became a clone of Paul.

The interesting point is that each philosophical/theological system affected the science that developed within it. Gnosticism gave rise to Aristotle and his incessant categorizing and measuring of everything. Nephishism gave rise to the big picture discussions – free from any need to measure anything. As you will see when we unroll it – the Theory of Relativity is, in fact, very Nephish.

- Western <u>science</u> grew out of Gnosticism, and its need to categorize and measure. It gave rise to a bottom-up, data-driven approach.
- Western <u>philosophy</u> came from Nephishism and it's need to ask "why". It gave rise to a top-down or top-to-top theory-driven approach.

The data driven approach fit hand in glove with the requirement that theory should be based on observable fact. It works like a charm – until you are working with things that are too small or too big to be observed by the senses. At that point, theory must depart from Aristotle's rule about material measurability. When things are impossible to see, feel and touch – you simply have to live in a world of:

- Theory-to-theory development;
- Surrogate phenomena; and
- Indirect and global measures.

Maybe it's time to award a Nobel Prize for Nephishism, because every single one of our 4 guests in this chapter were Nephish.

Luther flew at 50,000 feet, moving from one theoretical point to another in a stellar demonstration of the Socratic Method under combat conditions. He took no prisoners, and was perhaps the most crudely confrontational of any historic figure.

The same is true of Franklin, except for the crudeness part. In fact he was conscientiously humble and cordial in anything he wrote. But he too stayed at the theoretical level and moved from one big picture concept to the next, including things such as – is it more important for a government to provide actual justice or simply the appearance of justice?

Adam Smith was completely in the clouds – all the time. Is it possible to reform the individual's soul, or should we set up a system that turns self-centeredness into other-centeredness? Is the determinant of a king's wealth the gap between him and his peasants, or the gap between him and some other king? Is fairness based on proportionality or equality? Etc.

And you already know about Einstein and his Nephishistic, Jewish soul.

6

NEW IDEAS
(NAUSEA, RAGE AND ADJUSTMENT)

A tour through world history is always invigorating, but it leaves us with a "So What?" question. The old walls primarily matter as a means to understand the monumental quality of the new stuff each guy brought to the table. Think of it for a moment. Calculating the earth's orbit around the Sun is easy. It's just a measurement exercise. The monumental, brain-stretching, logic-defying, god-threatening discovery was that the earth <u>did</u> orbit around the sun. We'd always thought everything revolved around us (the classic ego-centric interpretation of the universe).

Now that's what you call a paradigm shift. Yesterday, we knew we were stationery and that the heavens moved in a slow and stately pattern around us. Today we found out that we are actually spinning on a thing called an axis at a speed of 1,000 mph, while hurtling through space in orbit around the sun at a couple million miles per hour. I feel suddenly nauseous, as though the earth had just shifted beneath my feet. That's Paradigm Shift.

Have you ever been sitting at a stoplight, or in an automatic carwash, when you suddenly realize you don't know whether it's you that's moving or the other guys? You remember that weird dizzy reaction you had? You remember the nausea? You remember the utter panic? That's the paradigm shift effect. It is utterly miserable.

That's why the world hates change. Every time it happens the world throws up … all over its new shoes. We hate change. Well ---- we actually hate the paradigm shift effect. We tend to adjust to the actual change itself.

2010 provided a classic example of this phenomena. America went into full battle mode over providing basic health care for sick folks. You'd think that it would have had universal support, for three compelling reasons.
- A healthy populace means a healthy workforce. A healthy workforce means more money circulating in the economy.
- The electorate voted Obama into office based on a platform promising this very change. It was no surprise. And he won a sizable majority of votes.
- We're talking about sick kids here. The milk of human kindness tends to wrap them in a warm PR glow.

Yet a sizeable number of people reacted as though shocked that such a thing could happen. The Tea Party stormed onto the national stage, and talk radio had a field day. This may prove to have been the last gasp of one generation's ultra conservative fringe. Or it may have been the final exit of civil discourse – and therefore compromise – from the American stage. If so, we're in real trouble. Paradigm Shift is monumentally important. Empires fall over such issues.

The Paradigm Shift about the sun was the work of Copernicus. But he never would have done it without Luther and Luther never would have done his thing without Columbus. And so it goes. One giant stands on the head of the ones who went before.

One of the more awe-inspiring paradigms of all time was produced by Creb, moger of The Clan of the Cave Bear. He came up with the concept of 2. Without him, Einstein never would have had a chance 7 million years later. Creb, you see, invented counting. That made him the true father of mathematics. Creb is also a fictional character, who stands in for the real but anonymous guy or gal who actually came up with the concept. If you haven't done so already, you'd be well served to run out and buy Jean Aul's book. It is a true gem of popular anthropology.

You need to be like Creb if you're going to be a vision-based leader. You need to invent (or discover, or realize) some version of the concept of two. A basic concept that is so simple, yet so profound, that it alters the world forever-after. Simple, yet profound. Keep repeating that mantra. That, in and of itself, is the core of the creativity part of vision-based leadership.

Keep your antenna up for that as you travel through the rest of this book. We're going to dissect our four main characters, take a look at their contributions and find out why they were so earth shaking.

In the process, we're also going to observe the power and perseverance it took to implant that guy's basic concept(s) into the psyche of the larger world. That's the 2nd component of vision-based leadership. And it's the point at which most visionaries fail. They can't overcome the wall - the forceful resistance that greets every new basic concept.

Once we've digested the creativity and power issues, we'll look for some commonalities in the lives of our main Creatives - to see if there is a pattern. If so, it'll give us a handle on the source of vision-based leadership, and thereby help us unlock it in ourselves.

The last section of the book offers a little advice about what to do with this gift once it blooms within you.

7

LUTHER'S NEW IDEAS
(STANDING EYE TO EYE WITH GOD)

After being in existence for 1,500 years, the Christian Church had finally established several core beliefs which it's members more or less all agreed to.

- There is a God
- He has a Covenant with us – ie - certain rules he wants us to live by (the "deal") and sanctions that incentivize us
- Eternal damnation goes to those who live outside the deal

- Eternal life (salvation) goes to those who live within the deal
- God sent Jesus, his only son, to update and finalize the deal
- Jesus conquered death via His resurrection
- If we accept all this we go to heaven

Regardless of whether or not you believe those things, you gotta admit – they're fairly straightforward. Everything other than that is just theological fine points. And like everything else in life, the details are what sink you.

1. The Church saw God as a moody god who was mostly angry and judgmental because of Man's incessant sinfulness. His chief joy was exercising his righteous indignation by condemning sinners to the eternal perdition of Hell – a place of torture and terror beyond imagining. And God was very personal. He saw and remembered what each and every person did and thought, and he was keeping score. So our behaviors were crucially important. Let's call it the "Doctrine of Works". You could buy your way out of a justly deserved visit to Hell by doing good things. This would mollify God for a while --- until your next screw-up.

   Luther responded by slamming his fist through a wall and roaring, "Bullshit!" Literally. The first thing you need to know about Luther is this --- he may have had an incredible intellect, but he also had the personality of a bar room bully, and the mouth to match. His articles and books are not for the faint of heart. In spite of this, Luther's theology, did not envision a moody God. Instead, God was consistent, controlled, ultimately benevolent. So Luther's God didn't hover and didn't keep score. He didn't even care that much about what we did. Instead he cared about what we *thought*. He had set the deal (The Covenant) in motion long ago, nothing had changed since then and all we have to do is say thank you, and we're in. Let's call it the "Doctrine of Grace". Among other things, Luther replaced terror with hope. That's what you call a new vision.

2. <u>The Church</u> also said that God wouldn't wait until the end of time to act on people's righteousness or lack thereof. Instead, He was constantly interceding in the here and now – through miracles and revelations.

   Luther was reluctant to acknowledge miracles or revelations, since they were not subject to logical step by step examination. This was key, since Luther believed above all else, that God was rational and logical. He knew this as fact, since Man was created in God's image, and Man had the faculty for logical examination. So if something could not stand up to the rules of logic, it clearly was not of God. A nifty piece of logic, don't you think?

3. <u>The Church</u> claimed that this salvation business was way too complex for the average guy to handle on his own. I mean, God has secret rules and you don't know them. There's magic involved, and you don't know that either. There's a complex and lengthy history behind all this, and you don't know that either. If you try to figure this out on your own, you're going to Hell on the express train. Luckily, God had shared these secrets with St. Peter, the only guy who was both sharp enough and brave enough to use them wisely. Those secrets were called the keys to the Kingdom. And Peter had told them to the 2nd Pope, who told the 3rd, and so on through all time. Each Pope would then educate his Cardinals, who taught the Bishops, and they'd give the priests just enough of the secret knowledge to help the peasants. But this was powerful medicine so the Pope and cardinals kept most of the secrets to themselves, lest Man harm himself with too much knowledge.

Luther, on the other hand, said Pish Posh (or some such sweet rejoinder). There were no mysteries. Anything God wanted us to know, He put down in straightforward black and white, in *The Bible*. We're just supposed to read it, understand it and apply it to our lives. In short, things run by immutable divine law – not by divine whim or magic tricks.

4. Not surprisingly, the Church invoked a bottleneck model of religion. Everything was funneled through the church. Mass was in Latin, and therefore indecipherable by the average peasant. *The Bible* was in Latin and therefore unreadable by anyone except the priest, especially since the general populace had sunk into general illiteracy by that time, even in their own language. The church also erected an intercessory wall between Joe six-pack and the almighty --- Mary, all the Saints, and the priest. You never approached God directly. They did it for you.

Luther, amidst a cloud of expletives, stated unequivocally that power over one's own soul should sit firmly in the hands of the individual, not the church. And this had more to do with his assumptions about God than about his opinion of Man. God is consistent, obvious and logical. Therefore, Luther had an open window model of religion. The average Joe could and should have a direct line to God. It turns out that God knows all languages, even yours. So Mass should be conducted in the language used by the local parishioners, and *The Bible* should be translated into every language known to Man, so that we might all read God's word in our own tongue, and judge for ourselves what God wishes. And for God's sake, teach the peasants how to read!

5. Next, Luther removed the intercessory wall, and informed folks that they could pray to God directly and give Mary and the Saints the day off.

6. Finally, he came up with an idea called "the priesthood of all believers" which effectively demoted the clergy. Since there was no magic, we didn't need the magicians. In its place, he set up rules of logic – straight out of his Socratic law books - for determining God's Will.

In short – Luther had three major beefs with the Pope

A. that grace, not works, was the key to salvation (a theological issue)

B. that the clergy possessed entirely too much power (a political issue)

C. that selling indulgences to pay the mortgage was an abomination (an ethical issue).

Now where have I heard that before?
You need to see this tussle between Luther and the Pope in perspective. The Church wasn't actually "the church". In fact, the organization Luther took on was only "½ the church". You see, it had been through all this once before, so by the time Luther showed up, it had shrunk to half its former size. Here's the story.

The Emperor Constantine paved the way for Christianity to become the official religion of the Roman Empire in 311 AD; ending forever its persecution and restoring all its property and assets. So after a very rocky start, Christianity moved from being an odd-ball sect of Judaism to being the faith of the mightiest empire in history. But before the church could even get settled into its new digs, the Emperor uprooted the entire core of his government and moved it to the little town of Byzantium, in 330 AD, where he built his new capital city – Constantinople – from the ground up.

Constantinople controlled the Bosporus Strait – the canal between the Black Sea and the Mediterranean Sea and was therefore the gateway to the riches of Asia. That's where the action was in 330 AD. Fifty years later, the bishop of Constantinople was declared to be the #2 bishop in the church – after the bishop of Rome, simply to throw a sop to those back in Italy. But everyone knew who the real #1 guy was – it was the bishop of Constantinople (the Patriarch). The Roman bishop (the Pope) was playing second fiddle.

The Constantinople church got most of the Emperor's time and money, so it was fabulously rich and powerful, with a glorious Cathedral, called Hagia Sophia, built in 537 AD.

For a full 1,000 years it was the most beautiful and largest cathedral in the world, which also made it one of the largest buildings in the entire universe. And to add insult to injury, the western church was forced to pay for a big chunk of it. That kind of wound leaves a scar. Meanwhile, the western empire had collapsed around the Roman Church and it was a mere also-ran in a world run by barbarians, and their pagan religions. The Dark Ages descended on Western Europe for 900 years and they were dark, in part, because the western church was pulling every string and sucking up to every local strong man it could – just to survive. Wise in the short run, perhaps, but it sowed some pretty nasty seeds for the long run.

After about 600 years, the western church had clawed it's way back to respectability and it tried to reassert the authority it never really had in the first place over it's prosperous eastern cousin. In 1054 the Pope tried to get the Patriarch and the Eastern Church to add a simple little 3-word phrase to their version of the Nicene Creed. The phrase was:

"... and the Son."

The Romans wanted to add it to the sentence "We believe in the Holy Spirit ... who proceeds from the Father (and the Son)". The Eastern Church saw this change as radical and sacrilegious. Therefore the Eastern Church saw itself as the protector of the Orthodox (traditional) faith – enter the Orthodox Church (Greek-, Russian-, Serbian – etc Orthodox).

The Orthodox Church rejected the Western Church's effort to control it and so the Pope and Patriarch rose up in rage and excommunicated each other – with full bombast and ceremony - somewhat like Dumbledore and Voldemort doing battle royal in <u>Harry Potter and the Order of the Phoenix</u>. Now that's what you call fighting over theological fine points.

       Very dramatic.
       Very emotional.
       And the church split in half on that day
         - never to be whole again.
       All over 3 little words.
       Three.   It boggles the mind.

The rift was so traumatic that Christian society took a nose dive again and for the next 400 years East and West repeatedly stabbed each other in the back --- and front, and raped and pillaged and murdered to their heart's content --- including a complete sack of Constantinople by the Pope's Crusaders on their way to fight the Muslims in 1204. History is a revelation, isn't it?

As fate would have it – those same Muslims finally ended the church's inter-Nicene warfare (so that's where the expression came from!) by conquering Constantinople in 1453. The Orthodox Church lay in ruins and the Roman Pope – God bless his hungry little soul – was finally the undisputed #1 ruler in the Christian world.

After taking about 50 years to consolidate things, the Pope finally decided it was time to give Rome a cathedral that would dwarf Hagia Sophia and thereby cement Rome as the undisputed head of the church.

That's St. Peter's Basilica, at the Vatican. So plans were laid and in 1517 the Pope's minions hit the trail, to raise money for St. Peter's mortgage by selling indulgences.

And that, of course, is precisely what triggered Luther's eruption; the same three issues as the Patriarch had had, 500 years prior.

1. Theological fine points, (this time "saved by grace, not works")
2. The power dynamics in the clergy, and
3. Mortgage payments

The Pope, who was tired of getting kicked around, declared "never again" and set out to eradicate this kind of thing once and for all. So he rose up in full bombast and ceremony and excommunicated Luther and condemned him to death. But somebody left a door unlocked and Luther literally snuck out the back, and the debacle of the Orthodox split repeated itself all over again. You'd think the church would learn quicker than that. Honest to God, you would. The only thing the Pope managed to do was shrink his church once again. So today it's about ¼ of the size it could have been.

And in 2007 Pope Benedict may have lit the match that will explode the Catholic Church once again, taking it to 1/8 of what it could be. In his push for purity of faith he reactivated the old Catholic doctrine that the followers of all other faiths are condemned to Hell, because Catholicism is the only true faith. That particular chestnut never has won friends for the church.

Who knows – maybe it's time for another Luther. Actually, there already has been a reformation of the Reformation. When the Swedes immigrated to America, they broke away from the Lutheran church and joined with the Congregational Church, or formed the Evangelical Covenant Church, or the Free church or … or … or … It just keeps reforming.

When Luther vaulted the wall and ran into the meadow beyond, he opened a vista to a new – unheard of – world. A world in which Man was worthy. He was worthy of God's benevolence and love. He was worthy to stand toe-to-toe with the almighty. He was able to read, and question and think for himself. He was able to impose the rules of logic on the real world as well as the mystical' and <u>reason</u> his way to faith, to knowledge, to his own personal handbook for the future. In short – Luther removed the yoke of terror, and gave man back to himself.

And once you realize you can question God, Himself; taking on the king is small potatoes.

❧

8

FRANKLIN'S NEW IDEAS
(DUMPING THE DIVINE RIGHT)

Luther invented a religion. That's a task of monumental proportions. Franklin traveled in the same rarified atmosphere. He invented a whole country, right before the eyes of the entire world. This is pretty heady stuff.

Remember that the Wall of Rationality which enclosed Franklin, and all of Mankind in 1776, was called "The Divine

Right of Kings". Based on the assumption that worms had more merit than the average man, it's rigid upstairs/downstairs ethos of social class held society in lockstep with the Will of the King, the penultimate member of the upper class. Everything flowed downhill, from God to the King, to the Prince, to the Duke, etc., on down to the lowest peasant. In essence, it was nothing more than a secular version of the model which Luther had defeated in the sacred world. Obviously, Man has an inherent eagerness to kneel. We fit so comfortably into models that tell us that someone else is bigger, better, stronger and/or smarter.

1. <u>The Divine Right</u> was built around the belief that the King determined what was right and true due to the special wisdom God had given him. Chief among these truths was that men were NOT created equal. There were those few meant to rule, and the vast majority which were meant to obey. God therefore put a burden of obligation on the common man of service, obedience and loyalty … just like a faithful dog.

Franklin, in gentle and humorous dialogue, went the opposite way. He said some truths were self-evident. They were true because they were true – not because a king declared them to be true. Further, he claimed that one of those truths was that all men were created equal. In short, God did *NOT* create an upper and lower class. And still further, a second self-evident truth was that the creator had bestowed certain unalienable rights upon the common man.. One of them was the freedom to pursue his own happiness as he himself (not the king) defined it. Franklin reached back 2,000 years for that one. It was straight out of Aristotle's mouth. In addition, Franklin tossed in two more obvious rights – life and liberty – without which it is impossible to pursue happiness. All by itself, those few claims were enough to throw the world into upheaval, because they single handedly removed the central pillar of civilization – not just in Western Europe, but across the entire globe as well. But Franklin was not done.

2. <u>The Divine Right</u> claimed that government was instituted by God Almighty, to enforce, protect, and express the rights of the King. Consequently, a just government derives its powers from the King, who got them directly from the hand and Will of God.

Franklin mounted a frontal attack utilizing home-spun good humor that pre-dated Mark Twain – but with the same sure eye for the kill zone that Luther had. God had nothing to do with the formation of government, Franklin said. He was too busy dealing with the mess that the Pope and Luther had created. Instead, the self-evident truth was that governments were created by men. And Man had come up with the idea as a way to secure the rights of each and every individual. As a result, and hold on to your seats for this one, as a result --- governments derive their just powers from the consent of the governed --- not from God, and certainly not from the king. Every king on planet earth felt his sphincter tighten. But Franklin still wasn't done.

3. <u>The Divine Right</u> had one last refuge. Regardless of his limits and shortcomings, regardless even of his rampant prodigious evil – no king could be removed or killed because he was ordained by God. Likewise, any attempt to change the government was sacrilege, because it was an insult to God, who personally instituted it.

Franklin pointed out that Man has the right to alter, abolish or replace anything which Man has made. Therefore, if a government fails to secure and safeguard the rights of the individual, then it is the right of those individual men to make a different one.

When Franklin vaulted the wall and ran into the meadow beyond, he opened a vista to a new - unheard of - world. A world in which Man was worthy. He was worthy to stand toe-to-toe with the king, himself. He was able to read, and question and think for himself. He was able to impose the rules of logic on the world around him, and <u>reason</u> his way to the unfettered pursuit of happiness. In short – Franklin removed the yoke of inferiority, and gave Man a future of his own making. In short, he finished the revolution which Luther had begun.

It makes my blood dance to think of it, because my grandpa, eight generations back – the Rev. Jonathan Edwards (of "Sinners in the Hands of an Angry God" fame) – had been Franklin's mentor on the role and responsibilities of individuals. So when Franklin (at age 70) took Thomas Jefferson (age 33) in hand and mentored the most important document ever written by Man – The Declaration of Independence*, a little bit of me was in that room. I like that. A lot.

The Declaration was the work of the "Committee of Five", appointed by the Continental Congress. Franklin turned down the job of being the primary author because he was afraid that his high profile life would bias the readers. John Adams stepped aside for the same reason. And that left Jefferson, who was the best writer of the remaining three members.

He took to it with relish, and gave vent to his pet issues - the rights of man, the limitation of government and the consent of the governed - which he had learned from a whole bevy of writers, including Locke, Mills, Rousseau and Francis Bacon.

---

* This is blatant jingoism, of course, and therefore an exaggeration. But we <u>can</u> make a case that it is among the top 10 most important documents ever written by Man. I still like that.

Then he wrapped it all in the empiricism championed by Sir Isaac Newton; the meticulous development of proposition, data and logic. Franklin took the first draft in hand, made around 50 suggestions, which Jefferson incorporated and sent to the Congress for discussion and approval. But there's something else you ought to know.

Franklin's Secret Weapon

Four of the five members of that committee belonged to something called The American Philosophical Society, a national society of the leading thinkers, patriots and moral philosophers of the day. Franklin had started it back in 1743, and its membership included not only Franklin, Adams and Jefferson, but also George Washington, Alexander Hamilton, Thomas Paine, James Madison and John Marshall. And Franklin had been the president of it for years. It was, in essence, the "Franklin University of Revolution." No wonder the rest of the founding fathers paid so much attention to Franklin. He's the one who'd taught them how to pull off this whole independence thing.

Oh Yeh – and one other thing.

He single handedly wrote the bulk of the U.S. Constitution 35 years before it was adopted. At the beginning of the French and Indian War in 1754, the British had convened a Congress of North American colonies to plot strategies for improving relations with the Indians and defeating the French. Franklin turned in a broad "Plan of Union" for all the American colonies. The British rejected it on the spot, but much of it was incorporated into the U.S. Constitution that was finally adopted in 1788. This guy was amazing. Let's take stock.
- Franklin was a self made millionaire by age 40
- He wrote the core of the US Constitution 35 years early
- He established a school for the founding fathers
- He was the midwife for the Declaration of Independence
- He single handedly got France involved on our side

- He negotiated the treaty of Paris which ended the War
- He was the glue that held the constitutional convention together.

And then there are my three favorites; justice, liberty and process

1. Justice ----

The Divine Right, being based on the Will of God, built it's justice system around discovering absolute truth and dispensing true and pure justice so that God's righteousness would hold sway in the world. Hence, the use of torture, indefinite imprisonment and summary punishments for surprisingly minor infractions. They were dedicated to finding the absolute truth, so they could live in strict accordance with God's holy will.

Franklin championed a less lofty mission. He just wanted to prevent vendetta and feuds. He proposed the novel notion that the system had to dispense the *appearance* of justice, not justice itself (which you where never sure of accomplishing, anyway). Hence the absence of torture, the writ of habeus corpus, the 5th amendment protection against self-incrimination. Franklin gave us the core of our legal system – the approximation of justice – which is a far more humane way to live.

2. Liberty -----

The Divine Right claimed that God wanted order above all things. And therefore, peasants needed to trade their liberty for the sake of safety, predictability and order. And since the average man fears uncertainty more than any other danger, it was an easy sell. This rigid code was based on the right to command & obligation to obey.

Franklin saw this as the most heinous legacy of The Divine Right, and he waged war against it his entire life. Perhaps his own favorite of his many clichés was "A man willing to give up liberty to gain a little safety is deserving of neither." That's the sentiment that inspired Patrick Henry – "give me liberty or give me death". The constitution is, in essence, a document dedicated to limiting government and maximizing individual liberty. You can thank Ben Franklin for that.

> A man willing to give up creativity,
> for a little safety,
> is deserving of neither

3. Process -----

The Divine Right was based on moral absolutes. There was a right and a wrong. The difference was clear. And since truth was established by God, as revealed to the king, any disagreement with the King was an attack on God and had to be eliminated, by battle or execution. The Ayatollah and the Taliban were not the first to run a regime based on morality.

Franklin disagreed. Instead of seeing the nation as a thing held together by morality and battle, he envisioned a nation held together by ethics and compromise. He was the champion of civil discourse, soft debate and functional trade offs that lead to livable solutions for everyone. For Franklin, patience was not a virtue. It was a tool. He is the one who taught us to hold our manly rage in check, schedule our revolutions every 4 years, and to shoot ballots – not bullets.

> Patience is not a virtue.

It is a tool.

I would propose that Ben Franklin is the true father of the U.S., and I thank him for it.

And now for an historical postscript
In response to the 9/11 terrorist attacks, the administration of George Bush II turned it's back on Ben Franklin, and his vision for America.

- Torture became a publicly acknowledged interrogation protocol of the United States for the first time in history.
- The writ of habeas corpus was suspended.
- P.O.W.s were reclassified as "enemy combatants" and prisons were located off shore – so that the administration could argue that they were unprotected by either the Geneva Convention or the US Constitution.
- Wrapped in the Flag, the "Patriot" Act removed a number of the safeguards of the Bill of Rights.
- And the President's nominee for Attorney General flatly refused to discuss whether an obvious torture technique, such as water boarding, was in fact a torture or just a moist way to say good morning.

Check the soil above Franklin's grave. I imagine it has been thoroughly churned from all the flipping he's been doing. I truly hope there is a heaven. The conversation between those two should be a humdinger. Franklin might even start talking like Luther.

9

SMITH'S NEW IDEAS
(WHO IN THE HECK ARE THE JONESES?)

Right from the get-go, Adam Smith was one of the more entertaining thinkers of all time. He was a moral philosopher who said, "Stop trying to make Man moral." Instead, just stop abusing him and let him be selfish. You do that on a level field, and his actions will improve, even if his morals do not. You gotta love a guy who thinks like that. He sounds like Hugh Hefner's tutor. Let's look at the specifics.

Defining wealth ----- Smith said stop looking at the gap between you and your peasants. Forget the gap between you and your peasants. The gap between you and your peasants doesn't matter. Slap. Slap. Slap. The thing that matters is the gap between you and the king of France. In other words, change your point of comparison. Sitting out here in the 21st century, this point is a no-brainer. But to a world with a 10,000 year tradition of starring at the peasant gap, this was a radical new perspective; just as amazing and unsettling as

Copernicus' shifting us from earth-centeredness to helio-centeredness. It made one nauseous. Everything else came out of this for Smith.

The mark of favor ----- Smith borrowed heavily from Jean Chauvin, whom you and I know as John Calvin, the founder of Calvinism, and pillar of the Presbyterian wing of the Reformation. Calvin pointed out that wealth is the mark of God's favor for everyone, NOT just for the King. Smith adopted this point from Calvin, then added his own twist, as follows.

Measuring wealth on the run ----- Wealth had always been measured by the amount of land and bullion held by the king. Literally. Held. Not used, not farmed, not rented, not loaned out at interest. Just held. Most of it unused. But at least the peasants didn't have their grubby little mitts on it. Wealth was measured by <u>resources at rest</u>. Smith slapped the king upside the noggin once again and pointed out that this was the most unnatural of arrangements, since man had "a natural urge to truck and barter", not to hoard. Wealth, Smith argued, should actually be measured by <u>resources in motion</u>. He called them "capital", and didn't much care whether the king ate them, served them, cut them up piecemeal and sold them, rented them or put them in a dress and sang to them. Just do something with them – especially the bullion. Rent it out. Loan it to the nobles and charge them interest, or invest in a brewery or a farm or geez --- loan some to the peasants and see what they can do with it.

Reassigning the peasant ----- The peasant had always been seen as a competitor to the king. The richer the peasant got, the poorer the king became, in comparison. Smith pointed out that the peasant wasn't actually a competitor anymore, since the only thing that mattered was the gap between one king and another. So from now on, the peasant was the king's chief asset for exceeding the wealth of the other king. All you had to do was …

Stop abusing the peasants ----- Instead of holding the peasant down, via ruinous taxation and outright confiscation, Smith told the king to stop abusing the peasant and actually help him grow more wealthy than Midas. First of all, take the pledge. Get your hand up. That's it. Say it with me "As God is my witness, I will never confiscate again." Doesn't that feel better? In the process, Smith cemented the concept of private property, safe from unlawful seizure. And that extended to a man's ideas as well as his land, or sheep or new shoes.

Invest in your peasants ----- Help them find better seeds, better farming techniques, better transportation systems, better storage and better marketing. Maybe even loan them money, or rent them your fallow land at a reasonable rate.

Tax them at a reasonable and proportionate rate. ----- That way, they can continue to get rich, and you get even richer, because you get a little chunk of every single peasant's money. And no one peasant will ever be richer than the king, because the law of large numbers will swamp him. Bill Gates may have his billions, but the US government has its quadrillions. The king wins! (If we had a king. You get the point.)

Redefining usury ----- It turns out, John Calvin had said, that God was not against loaning money at interest. He was only against loaning money at <u>exorbitant</u> interest. Smith liked this point as well, so he suggested that keeping interest at about 20% or less would keep God quite happy.

81

All by themselves, these 8 points would be an impressive life's work for any genius. With them, Smith had established a new way of life on planet earth.

- One based on merit, not on might.
- One based on interdependence, not unilateral abuse
- One based on mutual contribution.
- One based on a pie that could be enlarged

Think about that last one for a moment. In a stagnant economy, every baby born diminishes the wealth of everybody else since the pie has to be sliced thinner and thinner. But in an economy that can grow (because assets are circulating rather than sitting in the king's barn), each new baby holds the potential of growing the pie itself, because each person is a productive unit that adds something to everyone else. Smith was the penultimate positive mental attitude guy. He was Tony Robbins in knee socks and a wig. But he was offering substance and not just fluff. He opened the door to collective actions, from the formation of corporations, to banks to co-ops. He opened the door to widespread saving and investment.

But wait! There's more.

The Nature of Man ----- According to Smith, Man was not brutish, dishonest or lazy. Instead, he was perfectly rational, gifted with a reliable if-then logic at birth. It's just that he focused this rationality on his own self-interest, rather than on the welfare of others. In short – Man did not need to be reformed – just redirected. That one observation caused about 2,000 years worth of discourse and accumulated wisdom to collapse on itself, and carried us right back to Aristotle's knee, where we could learn once again that Man was on a quest – a pursuit of happiness … as defined for and by himself. It was almost as though Franklin, Jefferson and Smith were all cousins.

Specialization ----- The best way for Man to pursue his self interest was to specialize – find something he was good at, and do nothing else. And do it again and again. And pay attention to what he did. And figure out how to do it quicker, better, cheaper. And then improve it all over again. Say goodbye to the jack-of-all-trades generalist. The modern age would require everyone to be an expert in just one thing. And that would lead to prosperity, because specialization would lead to a formalized Division of Labor and organizational structure, which would lead to mass production which would lead to the development of both consumer and capital markets on the grand scale. But I get ahead of myself. Mostly, specialization led to want and plenty – otherwise known as …

Scarcity and surplus ----- If all I do all day, every day, is make straight pins, I will soon make far more of them than I need. I'll have buckets and buckets of the little suckers. But not a loaf of bread in the entire house; because I didn't take the time to plant the field, weed it, water it, chase away the varmints, harvest the crop, grind it, mix it and bake it. I was too busy making pins. Lucky for me, the woman down the street has been baking all day, every day for the past three years. She has tons of bread. But not a straight in sight. So specialization has created two conditions: We each have a Surplus, and each of us also has a Scarcity.

Trade ----- I could steal a loaf of bread. I could use the pins as a weapon I suppose. But what if her husband was a swordsmith? Hmmm. Perhaps there's a better way. I'll trade my pins for a loaf of bread. We'll screw things up at first, but over the next few weeks we'll figure out a fair exchange rate that we can both live with.

Supply and Demand ----- We could jerk each other around. I mean, she could demand 1,000 pins for a single loaf and laugh at my pain because she's the only baker in town.

But then young Bob down the street would get a bright idea one day and offer to bake for me for only 500 pins a loaf, and Marge (the original shrew who was screwing me over) would get religion and offer to do it for 400 pins. But she would be too late, because Bob had already made a couple loaves and I'd bought one for only 10 pins – because he was desperate to re-coup his costs. So Marge had to do the same or else the entire village would switch over to Bob. Now they are both mired in a state of self-imposed wage slavery --- until a guy from the next village over buys their entire inventory for 15 pins a piece and promises to do the same every Tuesday. Now we're back to starving again so we up the price to 25 pins per loaf to keep Bob and Marge from abandoning us. The peddler from the other village ups it a little as do we and soon we establish a stable price of 31 pins per loaf and we're all okay with it. Well, actually, we all feel like we're getting screwed – but only a little. That my friends is the Law of Supply and Demand, in living color – complete with an elegant demonstration of equilibrium pricing thrown in for free. Dismal science, my ass. This stuff is the bread of life.

The Invisible Hand ----- This is the part that my Republican friends love. Smith pointed out that government had no role in running this loaf and pin economy. No representative of the king established the cost, or the price, or who would make pins and who loaves. No body said the peddler had to be a peddler. No guild or union set the equilibrium price. It was all done by the magic of human self-interest. My self-interest bumped into Marge's and Bob's and the peddler's (I never got his name. Nice guy, though). And in order to feed my self interest I ---- well, let me have Adam himself tell you in his own words

"It is not from the benevolence of the butcher, the brewer, or the baker that we expect our dinner, but from their regard to their own interest. We address ourselves, not to their humanity but to their self-love, and never talk to them of our own necessities but of their advantages."

That's the Invisible Hand. That's the sacred stone that every Republican candidate has to kiss to have a chance. Get the government off our backs and we'll run this thing right ourselves. It's a policy called *Laissez-faire*. That has been the sacred mantra of the political right for a hundred years, from Ayn Rand, and Milton Freidman, to Neil Boortz and Rush Limbaugh. Newt Gingrich rode that pony to glory and rose to be the Speaker of the House and the arch-nemesis of Bill Clinton. But Newt, you knew better didn't you? You were a teacher before you were a politician. So you probably actually read The Wealth of Nations, in addition to just waving it in front of a TV camera. Shame on you. Here's what you left out.

The Guilds ----- First of all, Adam Smith wasn't so concerned about protecting the little guy from the government. Remember? He was writing this book *on behalf of* the government. He was trying to tell the government (the king) how to get rich! Hello. So who was he trying to protect the little guy from? The Guilds. The trade associations of and by business owners. They were strangling the economy with their restrictive trade practices, and price fixing. Again, I think it best to hear it directly from Smith himself.

> *"People of the same trade seldom meet together, even for merriment and diversion, but the conversation ends in a conspiracy against the public, or in some contrivance to raise prices. It is impossible indeed to prevent such meetings, by any law which either could be executed, or would be consistent with liberty and justice. But though the law cannot hinder people of the same trade from sometimes assembling together, it ought to do nothing to facilitate such assemblies; much less to render them necessary."*

Hmmph. That's kind of interesting. Don't you think?

The Level Playing Field ----- Smith knew that the Invisible Hand only worked on a level playing field, where all parties were equally empowered to secure their own welfare. And he put it right down there on the page in black and white so that everyone could read it for themselves. Maybe Luther was right. Maybe we should read things for ourselves. According to Smith, that balanced empowerment would come from any number of things; such as each party having:

- the ability to make or buy
- an alternate sources of supply
- complete knowledge of the market
- equal access to markets, labor, capital
- the ability to counteract the unfair practices of others

But, if the playing field became un-level, something would have to intervene to re-level it, or Capitalism would spiral into tyranny. Smith wasn't sure who or how, but 125 years later, Teddy Roosevelt would claim that task for the government, the only party big enough to counterbalance the full weight of a corporate cartel.

The Price of Civilization ----- That's what Ben Franklin called taxes. Everyone knew they were inevitable. The only questions were (a) who should pay them, and (b) based on what? Under the Divine Right, the king and nobles (the aristocracy) paid no tax whatever. They carried the burden of creating the peace and the enterprises that provided safety and jobs for everyone else. They'd already made their contribution to the state. So the taxes were paid by the peasants, often on a per head basis. Any attempt to tax the aristocracy had usually led to an insurrection and a dead king or two. So Smith proved himself to be a true radical by championing universal taxation. Everyone should pay them, according to Smith. And they should pay an amount proportional to their income.

In Summary

Luther invented a religion. Franklin, a country. Adam Smith invented a way of life; one driven and measured by the profit motive and regulated by the laws of supply and demand. And in so doing he took us back to the materialism of Aristotle and gave us a way to measure our progress on the quest for happiness. I am happier today than I was yesterday, because I bought a new car last night. That's how I know. I have more stuff.

It's not perfect, but it certainly has fueled an incredible outpouring of human creativity , ingenuity and hustle for the past 225 years, don't you think. Man has inhabited the globe for anywhere between 6,000 and 10,000,000 years. Even at the creationist estimate of 6,000 years, we can see that 95% of mankind's productivity has occurred in the most recent 4% of its days on earth. And the pace of innovation is increasing. We'd be hard pressed to argue that liberty and the profit motive weren't major factors in that explosion. And that's why I give Smith the accolade of having the most impact on the world. Not bad for an old Scottish guy who was a bit of a geek.

❧

10
EINSTEIN'S NEW IDEAS
(THE ART OF JEWISH SCIENCE)

For 99.9973% of his days upon this earth, Man has invoked God (or "the gods") as the explanation for just about everything. No wonder we made no progress at all. Everything was kept as a black-box phenomena. And no one was encouraged to look any deeper. Then someone invented farming and a creative surge followed. Man stopped migrating and invented villages, then wheels so you could get from one village to the next a lot easier, And Iron. That was a biggie. Man finally had a tool that was harder than mother nature. That's when man finally had enough free time to invent thinking. And he proved to be quite good at it.

Eventually, Aristotle came along and introduced materialism as a way to understand the world (ie – things happen because something material [concrete] triggers it --- not a mystic being). That's why Aristotle was so big on categorizing everything. If stuff is what makes things happen, then we better learn everything there is to know about stuff. Rationalism set in and for the next 600 years, civilization started to make enormous strides, in technology, in philosophy, theology, science and math. And engineering reached a level of sophistication that still amazes modern archeologists and architects to this day.

Then the Emperor quit on September 4, 476 AD and Rome fell. The curtain fell. The Dark Ages ensued, and Man went back to the black box – God makes everything happen, don't ask questions. Silence. For a thousand years. Think about that. A thousand years. Nothing changed.

Then Columbus makes his voyage,
Luther wakes up.
Copernicus points out that the Sun doesn't move,
and Isaac Newton becomes a knight for catching apples.

Science makes a comeback, the Enlightenment sets in, Franklin and Smith invent countries and systems and the world is overtaken by an hysteria for data. God is no longer the answer every time someone asks "Why?".

The Age of Empiricism ruled thought for almost the entire 1800s. And what a glorious time of materialism it was. Locomotives sprouted and crisscrossed vast continents. Telegraph provided instantaneous communication. Electric lights provided eternal daylight and the phone gave us a way to talk about it all. But nothing quite compared to that wonder of all wonders - the automobile. Within 100 years, Man had conquered Planet Earth; not by faith in an unseen God, but by the cool level-headed logic of the Scientific Method.

- Develop a hypothesis by meticulous inductive reasoning
- Gather hard data that can be confirmed by the 5 senses
- Analyze the data mathematically
- Look for alternate explanations
- Rework the hypothesis, or confirm it with a 2nd wave of hard data

Then Einstein appeared and violated every step.
That may actually have been his biggest contribution to
mankind. You see, the Scientific Method, itself, is a wall of
rationality.

Realize what was going on. You remember his critics? The
ones who called his work Jewish Science? Well, in addition
to the good clean fun of letting a little slander slide off the lip,
those critics were actually trying to prevent Man from sliding
back into the Dark Ages. Stay with me here.

- Science had just proven, once and for all, the undisputed
  superiority of data and linear logic.
- And all of this depended on a rock-ribbed rule. The data
  has to be material. I have to be able to verify it with the
  senses. I have to be able to hold it, physically count,
  weigh, measure, hear, taste or see it.
- No more mystic smoke and mirrors. This is the modern
  age!
- I therefore move from ignorance to brilliance by
  incremental steps, amassing and counting a few more
  beans at each stage.

It was a good system. It still is. In fact, it's still the mainstay
of education and research in the 21st century.

So why did Einstein abandon the Scientific Method?

Because the atom is too small. And because the universe is
too big. So Einstein couldn't measure, weigh, taste, much less
see most of the things he was discussing. No one could. So if
the core of your system is useless, the system itself is useless.
Therefore, you either abandon your inquiry, or you invent
another system.

Einstein chose plan B. He didn't start at the ground and work
his way up. He started at the top and stayed there. He was a

pure theoretician. He wasn't trying to make a better mouse trap. He was investigating the role of the mouse in cosmic history. To get a feel for this let's compare the analogies of two great minds

Newton would use a pithy little everyday example such as an apple falling from a tree to develop a major component of his grand theory. He'd note that it always falls straight toward the center of the earth. It never falls sideways. Wow! That's the law of gravity.

Einstein, on the other hand, would invent an impossible fantasy story called a "Thought Experiment" about Harry Potter on the platform for the Hogwarts Express. Hermione is already on the train and she is timing her trip with a laser clock she invented last year in Transformations Class. It periodically shoots a quanta of light from a point on the floor of her train car to the point on the ceiling directly above it. Hermione sees this as a perfectly vertical stream of light, because she, the train car, and the light are all traveling at the exact same speed horizontally.. But Harry sees something different, because he's not moving. Oh yeh – I forgot two details:

1. the train is traveling at the speed of light [that's 186,000 miles/second],
and
2. Harry's eyes and brain have the ability to register things moving that fast.

Obviously, Einstein was using a hypothetical story that was impossible to replicate in realty. But he'd blithely race along, simply assuming that of course, this type of thing happened everyday. He was like Jules Verne on speed. But hang on a second. What do you think Harry Potter would see?

He'd see a diagonal beam of light. Not a vertical one. Because in the time it takes for the light to go from floor to ceiling, the train car would have moved forward. Now what does that tell us? It tells us that from Harry's standpoint, time is slower on the train than it is on the platform. Congratulations, That's the Special Theory of Relativity.

- Einstein didn't use inductive reasoning to arrive at a hypothesis. He didn't start with the stress factors of rails and railroad ties, or friction coefficients of steel wheels, and work his way up, utilizing a complete literature review of all prior research.. He simply heaved Hermione onto a train and made up a story about her.
- He didn't even try to attach his story to anything remotely associated with reality.
- He didn't conduct an experiment because he couldn't. Laser clocks were a long way off, and trains couldn't go any faster than 100 mph. So 186,000 miles per second was a little out of reach.
- Consequently, there was no data that could be gathered. Forget confirming it with one of the 5 senses. He didn't even pretend. Hard data was simply unnecessary as well as impossible.
- Obviously, it was therefore impossible to do any mathematical analysis
- He was open to alternate explanations, but never saw one
- And he never confirmed his theory with a 2nd wave of data

Of course, Harry Potter wasn't around in 1905, so Einstein's work seemed even weirder then than it does today. Here's the point --- **Einstein blew apart a <u>double</u> wall.**

- **The wall that defined the world around us**
                    and
- **the wall that defined how we think about that world.**

He literally went back to his tribal roots. Not to Jewish science but to Jewish theology and philosophy; specifically to the school of thought called **Nephishism**, which - you will remember - sees the world as a fluid and constantly dynamic integration of all things, simultaneously. How else do you think he could come up with an idea such as time being bent. Or his discovery that space is NOT infinite, it just doesn't have any boundaries. If you want to keep up with Einstein you have to color outside the lines. There are no lines. Forget the lines. Slap, slap, slap. Just think.

What Einstein did was reintroduce the Inferential Leap to Science. On more than one occasion he said that his breakthroughs came to him in dreams. That was the easy part. The hard part was learning enough math to invent equations in reverse that would carry him back to a starting point where the rest of the scientific community could see where it came from. "I waste all of my time explaining things to smart people. They have the hardest time understanding."

I didn't know what it was called back when I first heard about Einstein's thought experiments. But I knew for a fact, with every fiber of my being, that the world made a lot more sense once I invented a train platform or some such thing in my head. I was in 6^h grade at the time and the world opened up before me with absolute clarity. But only for an instant. The problem I faced was that every teacher from that point until I got my PhD was an empiricist. They only knew how to think within the tight little world of the Scientific Method. As a result, I got semi-hammered into semi-shape so that I could sort of fit in a round hole, as long as someone kept chipping away at my pointy corners.

There were actually two guys in my personal history that kept a flicker alive for me. One was David Homcy, my English Lit teacher in 11th grade. The other was Zenos Hawkinson who taught the only history class I ever took in college. They both told stories. And then asked us what we thought about them. There was no one else, in all my years of school, who ever invited me to think. I'm grateful to Ed and Zenos. But what a sad commentary on the impact of an enormous wall in our lives.

I'm still pissed that I let myself get beat up for so many years. I just wasn't smart enough to create an Olympia Academy of my own. Einstein had done that with 3 of his friends. They made up the name, then sat around telling each other that they were right, and the world was askew. You need to hear that when you're trying to be creative. I didn't get that. So I was hammered every step of the way throughout my education, and especially once I started working for a living. What a miserable way to live. You get trotted out at cocktail parties to entertain the troops or an investor with your egg-headed idea of the day, then you get stuffed back in the closet as an embarrassment for the remaining 11 months, 28 days of the year. Eventually I gnawed off my foot and escaped. That's the story with most entrepreneurs.

Paul Simon wrote a song about Kodachrome pictures with a line that rings through the mind of every kid around exam time

> *"With all the crap I learned in High School,*
> *it's a wonder I can think at all."*

The crap isn't the content. The crap is the message that the only meaningful way to think about the content is the Scientific Method. We've created a couple generations of people who don't know how to take a quantum leap (which is, by the way a term from Einstein). That may be why Bill Gates had to drop out of Harvard to amount to anything.

The other awe-inspiring thing about Einstein was that he created another Copernicus Effect – you know - the Paradigm

Shift. We live in a world of space and time. And we use one to measure the other (as in miles per hour). And we know that space has 3 dimensions: height, width and depth. And we know that time has 2 dimensions: duration and intervals.

Based on the Theory of Relativity though, time and space have melded into a single concept – SpaceTime. And SpaceTime has not only the 3 dimensions of space and the 2 of time. It also has two other dimensions that are a result of the combination of the two: direction and speed. And then there were three more dimensions as well --- for a total of 10. And once you wrap your brain around that, it's not too tough to deal with the fact that time and space expand and contract as a result of changes in speed and that matter changes the shape of SpaceTime, which in turn moves matter. You'll get the general idea by thinking about a bowling ball in a 10 foot thick trampoline.

Another of Einstein's gems is the formula for wiping Man off the face of the globe

$$E = mc^2$$

It says that energy is the result of converting matter into motion. And since "c" is the speed of light, you can see that converting just a tiny bit of matter into motion has an astronomical impact. But here's the kicker. Other than the fact that Einstein saw the speed of light as the only constant in the universe, I still don't know how he figured that it was the multiplier. And I should point out that before $E = mc^2$ made any sense, he first had to prove that atoms even existed. Not bad for a day's work.

Then, of course, there is the known fact that Harry Potter is a troublemaker. So Einstein might have known he would put a spell on the train so that it left the tracks and moved about in any number of directions, while at the same time accelerating and decelerating in a random manner. Obviously, the special theory of relativity would no longer apply because we no longer have constant speed or direction. Damn!

So Einstein had to come up with the <u>General</u> Theory of Relativity – one that handled all velocities (speed & direction) and even worked on Sundays. He had to deep six the train platform thought experiment. In its place, he came up with the guy in the basket exercise. This guy's in a basket suspended in space by a rope, see, and he gets pulled rapidly (probably at the speed of light) in one direction and then in another, while also hurtling through space at some ungodly velocity (quick, someone guess "at the speed of light!"). And so we learn that gravitational mass and inertial mass are the same … locally. And we also learn that the things around your ankles are your pants. Belts pop at the speed of light. Of course, we never find out what exactly the basket is suspended from, nor do we find out what type of motor is used to pull the rope up and down at such a speed. But Einstein was not concerned with such pedantic details. The basket was the end-all and be-all. Anyways, Albert worked his way to general relativity and the age of inter-stellar travel was born. Man was no longer confined to earth. Before the Wright brothers even launched their first flight, Einstein had already mapped our path to Mars.

But most important – he mapped a different way to think about mapping a path to Mars. That, I believe, is Einstein's biggest contribution.

Unless you consider Quantum Physics.
Remember that story about light being a particle or being a wave? Well it turns out that a lot of folks think <u>that's</u> his biggest contribution. So here you have the science of the incredibly large, unlocked by the same guy who unlocked the science of the incredibly small.

Now that's a trick. And here's an interesting sidelight. The wave theory of light also had another enormous impact on physics. It moved it from mathematical analysis to statistical analysis, because quantum theory cannot predict exactly where light will show up. Remember, it's not just a particle, it's also a wave (it's a quanta – sounds like a breath mint commercial). So the best you can predict is the frontier along which the quanta might show up and then figure the probability for each point on that frontier. If you're not a science geek, this is hurting your head. I've been studying it for a while now, but it still gives me a furrowed brow. So let's back our way out of the science part. Suffice it to say that Einstein had to help develop a new type of math (quantum mathematics) to be able to talk about his new science, just like Newton had to develop calculus to talk about his new, mechanical world.

Wait, wait, wait!

There is one more mathematical thing I need to lay on you. I know I promised you, but this is too good to miss. Here it is. Einstein is the guy who intellectually moved us into a 3-dimensional universe. Before him, we still thought and calculated as though the world were only 2-dimensional. Einstein shifted our perspective (yeh, that's a 3rd or 4th paradigm shift we have to credit to him) not only via the theories themselves but also via the mathematics he used to describe them. You see, the Special Theory of Relativity didn't really need a lot of math to support it. But the same was definitely NOT true about the General Theory of Relativity. It needed a LOT of math. And a very special kind of math --- non-Euclidian Geometry. This is where it gets good!

Euclid invented geometry back in the days of the ancient Greeks. It's been around for ages. One of its major components is the triangle. We know that the three angles of a triangle always add up to 180 degrees. Always. That's the definition of a triangle. Three intersecting straight lines will always enclose a finite and defined space that has three 'corners", the angles of which will always add up to 180 degrees. Oh yeh?

- Draw a line from the North Pole, through London (which sits on the zero degree line for longitude) down to the equator.
- Now draw a line from the North Pole, through New Orleans (which sits on the 90 degree line for longitude) down to the equator.
- Now connect the two spots on the equator
- Congratulations, you've drawn a triangle
- If you could do it on a flat world map, you can verify with a compass that the angles add up to 180 °.

But if you do it on a globe, the angles add up to 270 degrees! Verify it for yourself. Every angle is a right angle (90 degrees). <u>That's</u> non-Euclidian geometry. I've been studying that for a while too and, in all honesty, I cannot comprehend people being able to think like that for long stretches.

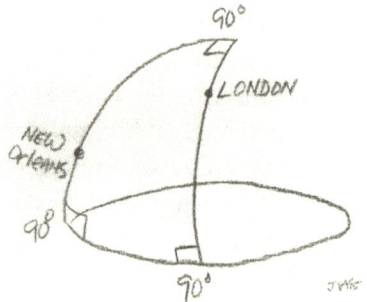

I'll tell you one thing, though. I don't think non-Euclidian geometry is fully developed yet. That's because there is no limit to the number of dimensions that the universe can take on. And as Einstein demonstrated, when you add a dimension it interacts with the other dimensions and they create more dimensions. Those suckers are breeders! Perhaps artificial intelligence is truly a possibility.

So where does that leave us?

Luther invented a religion. Franklin a country. Smith a way of life. And Einstein taught us to color outside the lines. Even if you never understand his theories, you can take that last point to the bank.

The world is different, vastly different, because of these four gentlemen. But the specific individuals aren't the key point here. I could have used Copernicus, Jefferson, Roosevelt (Teddy) and Alexander Graham Bell instead; or four others, or yet again four others. They would have worked just as well.

In fact, Roosevelt and Jefferson were on the first guest list. I replaced them because two other guys had the exact narrative ammunition I wanted to incorporate.

So the secret to creativity does not lie in these specific 4 people. They are arch-types --- stereotypes of the creative person. They are actually interchangeable. Isn't that a hoot?, These irreplaceable, incredibly important and absolutely unique people are actually interchangeable. I can hear Luther swearing at the thought.

What we're looking for here is a pattern, some commonalities that they all share. If we grab that, we may just have our tiger by the tail.

11

EXTERNAL COMMON GROUND

What's the source of creativity? I think it's nature – i.e.- we're born with it. But I could be wrong. So we're going to take a look at the possibility that environment has a major impact on the development of creativity as well.   We always find interesting things anytime we wander off the beaten path.

Luther's World

Right off the bat, I was struck by how similar Luther's world was to my own. On the day he hammered the 95 theses on the cathedral door, Europe was in the midst of a constant but slowly developing war with the Muslims. The Byzantine (Eastern Roman) Empire had just been conquered by the Ottomans 60 years before then, and the Ottomans were on the verge of making an all out attack on Vienna. In our terms that's like living in between World War II and now, isn't it? Especially when you remember that the Soviet Empire collapsed just a few years ago. Hmmmmm

On the one hand, the fall of Constantinople was a good thing for the Pope. His biggest nemesis, the Patriarch of the Orthodox Church had been reduced to mumbling in the dust and Rome was at long last the undisputed head of Christianity. The only downside was that the administrative burden on the Vatican suddenly exploded, as they scrambled to pick up the fractured pieces of the Orthodox Church.

On the other hand, the Muslims made no bones about the fact that Constantinople was just the beginning. Their real goal was to conquer all of Europe. And Europe didn't stand a chance due to the moral superiority of the Muslim faith. In the face of an adversary who is driven by absolute religious doctrines, the response is usually to fire up the absolutes on your own side of the fence as well. As a result, the Catholic Church was becoming even more doctrinaire than usual.

Side Bar

As you may remember, Pope Benedict did the same thing in 2007, with his declaration that the Catholic faith was the only route to salvation and eternal life. That was a doctrinal defense against modern day Muslims. But in the same breath, he was condemning a whole lot of Protestants and Jews to the eternal flames of Hell. Being a protestant, I do hope that God disregards the pronouncements of a Pope.

In addition to the religious upheaval, politics was also in transition. It seems to be a law of nature that whenever an empire ends, the world experiences a vacuum. Upheaval usually characterizes the ensuing years, which end with a new Empire getting sucked onto the world stage as a replacement for the old one.

In 1517 the world was headed for one of these cataclysmic confrontations between empires. In preparation for that battle, the Holy Roman Empire – basically modern day Germany – was pulling away from the Pope, in a move to become just the German Empire. You remember Columbus' Lost Generation? The ones that were 35 years old in 1517? Not all of them were peasants. Some grew up to be princes, dukes and earls. They'd taken over the reins of government by then and they were downright iffy about the whole omniscience and omnipotence claims of Mother Church. So they were getting ready to cut the apron strings.

- If the Ottomans went after Rome directly, the Germans didn't want to get sucked into the ensuing battle.

- If the Ottomans came after them, they didn't want to have Rome siphoning off their resources.

- And if the Ottomans didn't attack anyone – hey, that would be okay too. Then we'll just be paying taxes to ourselves, rather than sending them to Rome.

Besides, the nobles didn't have any clearer notion of what to believe in than the peasants did. In addition, Luther's world had a runaway form of communication that was too fast and too widespread for scholars to edit or governments to control. So the minds of the common man was being filled with pornography, unbridled political nonsense and outright slander.

It was the printing press, and by the
time Luther hit the scene it was 50
years old and in its prime. In our
day it is the Internet. And now that
WEB 2.0 is here – every person on
earth is a producer as well as user
of information. Unbridled.
Unedited. Pornography. Political
nonsense.

Outright slander. Luther would be right at home in Chicago,
2018. And lest you feel too comfortable, let me point out that
the Internet was first coming on line in the late 70s. That
makes it right around 30 years old today. Hmmm. I'm not
sure if those factors created Luther's creativity, but they
certainly kept him alive so that he could practice it. There
were any number of German nobles who were happy to keep
him hidden, and the general peasantry was happy to give him
safe passage. He was a German patriot, striking a blow
against the oppressive Roman colonizer. Hmmm.

In addition, Luther was exposed to a much broader range of
thought than the theologians of any prior generation – because
of the printing press. And I can guarantee you that most of it
was far randier than that produced by hand in the monastery
sweat shops. If nothing else that might account for Luther's
gutter-mouth. He sounded a like a gangsta rapper would
sound in church today. Hmmm.

As I sit here pondering it, it appears to me that the world
around him did have an effect on him, after all. If you study
Luther's work, what shows up time and again, constantly in
fact, is his unbridled rage against the self proclaimed
omniscience and omnipotence of the Catholic clergy. It's
Pavlovian. You say "Papacy" – he froths at the mouth (yeh –
complete with obscenities). His anger, in fact, was way out of
proportion to the issues he was confronting – almost like the

rage of a child when first he realizes that his father has been lying to him about the way the world works.

Here's an interesting thought --- Luther was the original "Lost Boy". He was <u>part</u> of Columbus' Lost Generation. Up until this moment in time, I've been developing an image of Luther standing outside the Lost Generation and preaching to it. I don't think that's true. I think <u>he</u> was as lost as the rest of them. That would certainly explain his youthful fling with the most severe vows of self-denial and self- punishment before discovering the doctrine of Grace. It would explain his suicidal despair. He was simply bashing around the world, wildly searching for something to believe in. And it would certainly explain his rage at the church hierarchy – the buffoons who pretended to have omniscience and therefore omnipotence as well. If the old Truth no longer rang true, Luther would just have to create a new Truth, or kill himself in the attempt. Columbus, you son of a gun. Hmmm. Maybe there's something to this environmental influence thing. Here's a thought.

- Maybe <u>you</u> are the new Luther.
- Maybe your neighbor is.
- Why don't you both get busy and find out?

Franklin's World

The Divine Right had one other cute element – Primogeniture. The oldest son inherited everything. The other sons got a peanut butter sandwich and best wishes for a useless life. The American Colonies were therefore built by England's 2nd sons. The lucky ones had scraped together enough money to buy a ticket; the rest became short-term slaves (7 years of less) to earn their passage. For 150 years, that's who came here. The second sons. And the second daughters, who could only land a second son. But after 150 years, they no longer identified themselves as the second sons of British estates.

No. They were a new thing altogether. They were the 1st sons of their own estates. You think those people had something to prove? Hell hath no fury like a woman scorned – except for a second son with 10 acres of his own.

Here's a bulletin for you. Ben Franklin had been a slave. His own brother had owned him. It was the British apprentice system. During your apprenticeship, you had the official standing of a slave, and the freedoms and rights to match. So Ben was apprenticed to his own brother in his printing business – and it offended Ben on several levels, not the least of which was the fact that he was demonstrably smarter than the dolt that owned him. So Ben ran away, and spent the rest of his long life with a warrant for his arrest trailing along behind him. He was a runaway slave. Something like that has an effect on a man.

During his escape by boat, Ben talked his way into a new job by charming one of the other passengers with his breadth of knowledge and rapier sharp wit. You see Ben had been reading all those things he was supposed to have been printing. He'd put himself through "school" on his brother's nickel. No wonder the dolt had made his life miserable.

One other thing. These Americans, these super men that surrounded Franklin, were doing something that no one in human memory had done before. They were literally carving civilization out of a vast untamed wilderness, at the speed of light. Starting with absolutely nothing, they had grown a burgeoning continent of several million moderately-educated citizens, complete with modern cities and transportation *in less time than it took to build a cathedral back home*. If you're part of the group that is accomplishing that kind of miracle – how likely are you to take orders from a demented king eating bon-bons back in London? I'm willing to bet that Franklin's love of liberty, belief in the common man and unbridled optimism had something to do with that experience.

Smith's World

Smith's world was the mirror image of Franklin's. The Americas were literally sucking the energy out of England. It was the hot place to be. So by Smith's time it was no longer the second sons who were slinking off to the American colonies. It was the cream of the crop, sailing first class.

The 1st sons were moving out. And as the ruling elite watched the wealth of the colonies grow they felt the gap between them and their peasantry shrink and they reacted in old school fashion. They tried to shrink the peasant's wealth, through heavy taxes, through confiscation, through limitations on the industries that could be established. They tried everything they could to slow the American deluge, but the damned stubborn colonists refused to live within reasonable limits. So every year witnessed a little more coercion from the king.

But these Americans who no longer saw themselves as second sons, no longer saw themselves as peasants either; and certainly didn't see themselves as, first and foremost, being English.

So Smith hustled into the role of the little Dutch boy, sticking his finger in the dike. When he was counseling the king not to abuse the peasants, he was making a last ditch effort to get him to stop abusing the colonies. But it was too little too late. By the time he published The Wealth of Nations bullets were already flying and the American colonies were a thing of the past.

Sometimes the best ideas come too late. If he'd just started that book 1 year earlier, he might have saved a huge chunk of the empire. But he didn't, so he didn't. That may be the main reason we play "Hail to the Chief" rather than "God Save the Queen".

Einstein's world

Time is the core of Einstein's work.

- The speed of light (miles per **second**).
- Velocity (miles per **second** x direction).
- The laser **clock**.
- Acceleration (change in miles per **second**)
- Constant speed (miles per **second**)
- $E = MC^2$ (C= the speed of light ... you know - **time**)

Now consider this. Before he was a world famous physicist, Einstein was just plain old obnoxious. He was whiney and argumentative. He challenged authority and generally ignored rule and edicts. He even relinquished his German citizenship because they were too militaristic. In his own words, he was an obnoxious Jew in an anti-Semitic land. His own professors wouldn't even recommend him for a teaching job after he graduated ... from a teacher's college.

This is absolutely pertinent information. It explains the wonders of his originality, which we'll talk more about later. But most important at the moment is that it offers an explanation for the role that time played in his scientific work. Being an obnoxious Jew is what introduced him to the clock.

You see, in order to support his wife and family, he took a job as a clerk in the Swiss patent office; the only position his few friends could scrounge up for him. And guess what his specialty was. He was the agent in charge of patents pertaining to clocks. That may not seem like much today, but at the time, that was a crucial function. International travel had become an everyday occurrence due to the recent development of a transcontinental train system. But the train schedules were undependable because the clocks were not synchronized. At the same moment in time, the clocks in Paris might read 32 minutes after the hour while the clocks in Prague read 17 minutes after the hour. This is not a problem, of course, unless you're traveling from Paris to Moscow by train and need to make connections in Prague at exactly 21 minutes after the hour. And if you miss them, you have to spend two days in Prague waiting for the next train, which gets you to Moscow a full day after the meeting that was supposed to avoid World War I.

You get the point. It was like screwing up the flight schedules at O'Hare Airport. Whole countries could grind to a halt. So how do you synchronize numerous static time positions with a thundering projectile hurtling through space? You bring the sum total of your extensive research to the patent office in Zurich, because Switzerland is the center of the time keeping industry for the civilized world. And you lay it before the avuncular little clerk named Einstein, and he compares it with all the other inventions and processes and their supporting data.

It is fair to say that after a couple of years, Einstein knew more about the practical aspects of time than any other single person on the face of the globe – by using the best engineering minds in Europe as his unpaid research assistants. Not only that - nothing got ok'd without his approval. He was, in a very real sense, the time master of all Europe. You think that had any impact on the focus of his scientific work?

Now ask yourself this; if you are already an outcast because you're Jewish, black or female, what more do you have to lose by also challenging the secular messiah – Isaac Newton, himself. Freedom's just another word for nothin' left to lose (thank you, Janis Joplin).

Reflections on the World
This brings us to an interesting sociological point. The PC school of thought bemoans discrimination as a terrible drain on society, because we rob ourselves of the rich diversity of

other cultures and perspectives. Let's take a look at that assertion.

From the individual standpoint, discrimination is clearly a terrible and humiliating thing to go through. But it is, frankly, hard to see how society suffers; especially when we compare the productivity, crime and mental health statistics of the ethnically, religiously and culturally uniform Japan, with the same statistics from France, England and the United States (three very diverse countries).

In addition, Janis Joplin opened our eyes to a positive, though unintended, result of discrimination --- it breeds creativity. Anecdotal evidence suggests that all other things being equal (education levels, access to information, food, shelter etc) the minorities, which are peripheral members of a society, seem to be the source of a disproportionate amount of creativity in that society. I will call it the Joplin Effect. You're welcome to join me. The "Joplin Effect". Sounds almost official, doesn't it. And consider this.

- Luther was the ultimate peripheral. He'd been excommunicated <u>and</u> sentenced to death, by the Pope.
- Franklin was a runaway apprentice, broke and the 15th of 17 kids – talk about marginal.
- They had been "Joplined".

Clearly, the world has a way of deriving benefit from us regardless of what we do to each other. It's almost as though Man was intended (or maybe just hardwired) for something good and noble despite his shortcomings.

In addition – note that technology caused a warp in space and time preceding each creative surge. Columbus expanded the size and complexity of the world 10 fold, but the printing press speeded up our ability to communicate with each other, thereby compressing time.   Luther therefore blossomed in the midst of a SpaceTime warp. After that, familiarity and nautical innovations shrank the world while the complexity of transatlantic communication slowed communication, providing Franklin and Smith with a SpaceTime that had doubled back on itself. Then the wonder of the modern train system arrived and shrank the world even further, while the wonders of the phone made communication instantaneous. And as they shrank, in tandem, they created an intellectual black hole, which sucked the genius right out of Einstein. Perhaps over-dramatized a bit, but a valid point none-the-less.

Technological change triggers
enormous waves of creativity
in its wake.

Then there is this ---
In addition to the instantaneous and uncontrolled communication media in Einstein's day, the world was crumbling.

- The family based dynasties of Europe were coming unraveled, as family squabbles erupted repeatedly into transcontinental wars that devoured the peasant class as cannon fodder for a new generation of hideous weapons of mass destruction. It was like a replay of the Greek Gods in Socrates' day.
- Not surprisingly, a new Lost Generation developed and loudly embraced bohemianism, anarchy and socialism as viable ways to order society and personal lives.

There's this social flywheel that seems to hum in the background for each of these four gentlemen. It sounds like the description of society at the point of each of the other three creative explosions. It's kind of eerie.

Finally, it should be noted that necessity is the mother of invention.

> Luther saved Columbus' Lost Generation from a Church that was spiritually corrupt and desperately resorting to wanton violence and smarmy pap to prop itself up.

> Franklin held together several million people during their fragile transition from colony to nation, in the face of superior military forces.

> Smith tried to race against time to save an empire that was clearly slipping away.

> And Einstein was battling for pure and simple truth in the face of the Newtonian's vain attempt to prop up a theory that was coming apart.

Each in their own way was pressed forward by the Leviathan that defined their world – the wall that surrounded them, encased them, smothered them.

So I am now converted. Of course environment affects Creatives. It determines, in part, who they become, what they see, how they work, what they value and the risks they are willing to take. That was kind of interesting. I'm going to take a break now. I'll get back to you in the morning

❧

12

INTERNAL COMMON GROUND
(THE DEMONS AND ANGELS WITHIN)

Environment is not the only thing that affects creativity. Internal factors seem to be in operation, as well. So we will turn our attention from Nurture to Nature at this point and see if there are any common threads that run through the makeup of Creatives.

Searching for the Renaissance Man

My life changed when I was 5 years old. My folks took us to Monticello that summer, Thomas Jefferson's home in Charlottesville, Virginia. Jefferson was a true Renaissance man – a Jack-of-all-trades with a curiosity that seemed limitless. He had a cannonball clock, and a mangy old buffalo head in the foyer of his otherwise pristinely proper colonial mansion, and he was a noted success in many fields. He was a noted horticulturist and architect. He was a respected archaeologist and paleontologist, author and inventor, statesman, President and founder of the University of Virginia. He did more in the average day than most people did in an entire year.

That was my first exposure to a Renaissance man, and I decided right there, on the spot that I was going to be one too.

I even remember where. I was standing in his bedroom, staring through his built-in canopy bed into his study. I was intently studying the globe by his desk when I made the commitment.

And I have known ever since that the breadth of the Renaissance man was a necessity for creativity. Jefferson proved it, as did Copernicus – who did a little of everything. He was an astronomer, economist, lawyer and physician, as well as being a catholic priest. Isaac Newton was a theologian, lawyer and alchemist. Being a physicist was the 4th thing on his list, maybe even 5th. He was also the kings' lawyer.

Teddy Roosevelt was very much the same. He'd been a boxer, a cowboy, a soldier a taxidermist, a conservationist, a hunter and the President that dragged this country into the realm of first world nations. Oh yeah – he also built the Panama Canal and won the Nobel Peace Prize for brokering an end to the Russo-Japanese War.

These guys had been on my original list of Creatives that changed the world. I was doing quite well in compiling a wealth of anecdotal evidence to support my contention. Even Einstein had multiple vocations: time master, sailor, hiker, inventor, scientist, and professor. And Luther, well, he was all over the map: monk, priest, pastor, preacher, professor, and writer.

Franklin, of course, was a world class Renaissance man – so masterful in so many fields that he is officially listed as a "Polymath" – a super Renaissance man – as are Newton and Jefferson as well. But I believe Franklin has become my favorite. He was the inventor of marvelously useful products such as swim fins, bifocals, heating stoves and lightening rods. He was the leading theoretical scientist in the field of electricity. He was a newspaper baron, a best selling author, an environmentalist, diplomat and public relations wiz. He was a political theorist and politician of surpassing acumen. And he was the subversive genius who educated the political leaders of the revolution.

Then I bumped into Adam Smith. He was a geek. I studied him from every angle I could, but nothing. He was a moral philosopher, author, tutor, and professor. But that's what you have to do if you're a moral philosopher. You're not qualified to do anything else. So Smith was a single-focus geek. A toolie. As I pondered that, I realized that Einstein was actually a geek too. He sailed and hiked as a hobby, not as an avocation. The closest alternative career skill he had was music. He was a pretty fair violinist, with a love for Mozart, but never went beyond the parlor. And as I pondered further, I finally had to admit that the same was true of Columbus and Luther as well. The various positions they held were just normal progressions in their primary vocation.

So that blew a hole in my theory. The truth is that you <u>don't</u> have to be a Renaissance man in order to be a Creative. It sure seems to help, but it's not required.   Rats!

The Id
When not busy calling one pope or another out to the alley for a well deserved ass kicking, Luther was so consumed by "the fire" that he renounced his priestly vow of chastity and married a nun.

Franklin joyously kept a stable of women happy, both in and out of wedlock, (they were in and out of wedlock, not him). He embraced each one as a special treasure, and by them sired several children without benefit of clergy – one of whom grew up to be the Governor of New Jersey and an avowed enemy of his – except that they visited each other periodically during the war.

114

Jefferson is widely known to have relieved the stresses of office in the warm embrace of Sally Hemmings, his negro slave, at the same time that he was lobbying for the abolition of slavery.

Einstein shacked up with his own cousin while his wife was living out of the country, and then apparently took a liking to his niece as well. There survives a letter in which the cousin in question lets Einstein know that if he prefers her daughter as a bedmate she will step out of the picture and let them live happily ever after. Einstein, of course, did the noble thing (if nobility there be in such a situation) divorced the wife and married the mom (his cousin) – who probably spent the rest of her life looking over her shoulder at her daughter (the niece).

And why would his first wife relinquish him – he being such a gem? She kept refusing, until he bribed her with the winnings he would one day obtain from a Nobel Prize, somewhere in the iffy future. They were both so sure he would win, that it was not seen as a risk by either of them. She took the money; he bagged the babe … or two. And you think soap operas are absurd.

Then, of course, there's Adam Smith, who spent a fair amount of his adult life being the private tutor for a string of young boys as they toured the continent. He may have been gay, but we simply don't know for sure. Great men always demand that their papers be burned upon their death, knowing full well that a museum will get them instead. Smith was different. He actually burned all of his personal papers, himself, during his last year of life. One wonders what he was covering.

We do know that he never married, and lived with his mother until she died – only 6 years before him. His contemporaries described him as a gentle, absentminded bachelor gentleman with "peculiar habits of speech and gait" and a distracted and far away look in his eye. Sir Isaac Newton had been much the same.

Now, before you jump to the conclusion that men are sexist pigs, let me hasten to point out that the same behavior seems to show up in female Creatives. Madame Currie, at the height of her fame, was in frequent correspondence with Einstein; not on the topic of Physics, but in exchanging advice on how best to hide and exploit the extramarital affairs each was having.

Here's the point. Each of our four guests had a raging Id. And it carried them outside the acceptable norms of their own culture. If you read back through the biographies of Creatives, you will find peccadilloes aplenty. In fact, I would hazard a guess that non-traditional sexual proclivities are one of the few common factors in all Creatives. In the most intimate and private part of their lives, each was free of strictures that bound those around them.   One even wonders if there is a cause and effect relationship here.

I have an idea. Why don't you become empiricists? Take a few steps outside the box. Break a few taboos. Embrace them, wash in them, glory in them. Then pay attention to what happens to your creative output both in terms of quantity and variety, not to mention quality. Remember – it's for the sake of science. Send pictures.

The Ego
Another characteristic that all Creatives seem to share is Ego. Luther was a raving egotist, taking on the Pope, church and the forces of Satan in a very personal war. Eventually, I believe, it drove him over the edge. Much of his later work exhibits signs of paranoid schizophrenia, peppered with delusions of grandeur and pathological rage. At a minimum, we'd have to say his egotism created several anger management issues.

Franklin, on the other hand, was a loveable and endearing egotist. He embraced it merrily, and instructed his son in writing (and therefore the rest of the world) on how to travel in the sheep's clothing of feigned humility.

Smith was an elitist, an intellectual snob.

And Einstein was a wide-open egotist, rivaling Franklin, who craved fame and turned everyone around him into his personal valet by always being late, disheveled, disorganized and distracted. It's a standard passive/aggressive tactic for taking control of relationships.

To some degree or another, the same seems true of every other Creative in history. Apparently, it requires an unseemly amount of self-confidence to battle the gods.

The Superego

Another thing that struck me is that each and every one of these guys had a fire in his belly – some overarching value that carried them obsessively on through thick and thin (can I say that without sounding hackneyed and trite)? Yeh, I can. Thick and thin

- For Luther it was a vision of men with self esteem worshipping God out of hope rather than fear.
- For Franklin it was the honest- to-god dream of a nation of enlightened citizens, able to govern them selves in fairness and honor.
- For Smith, it was the mission of establishing a cultural system that would redirect the beast rather than try to reform him – like cultural judo. And
- for Einstein, it was a burning desire to discover and tell the truth, like a scientific Columbo. He never gave up. Never.

Every single one of these guys was driven by something outside themselves. Something altruistic. Something for the good of mankind. The Id may free them, the Ego may fire them up, but the Superego is what steers them. Son of a gun. Freud was right! This stuff fits together, doesn't it? That's probably why he's also on my extended list of Creatives who changed the world.

Mental Health

Our brief pass through these four biographies confirms what considerable medical research has found. Manic/Depression, now known as Bipolar Disorder, is the handmaiden of creativity. It may be possible for an innovator to be constantly productive and upbeat, but a Creative operates on a flywheel cycle. There are times of intense, obsessive productivity, followed by predictable troughs of morose uselessness.

For some, such as Luther, the swings are extreme; from the joyous bloodlust of xenphobia to soul crushing suicidal lethargy. For others it is moderate; from finger snapping, foot tapping productivity to no worse than introspective melancholy. But all of them follow this cycle, what Einstein's cousin/wife called "creative eruptions".

Einstein and Franklin were for the most part joyous about their condition. They found it a friendly companion and useful aid. Smith accepted his fate, grimly. Like everything else, though, the condiditon enraged Luther. It insulted his neat, if-then linear logic. It seemed somehow mystic, which was the very thing he was fighting.

In point of fact, for many Creatives, what we call mental illness is what they call their muse. They embrace the myticism as a gift from the Creator. Not surprizingly then, most Creatives vehemently fight against any effort to "cure" their problem. They are more than willling to suffer the hell of the low for the unearthly rush of the high.

I can tell you from first hand experience that there is nothin on planet earth that compares to a creative high. The entire universe fits together into a synergistic whole. You could map the entire genome with one hand tied behind your back – while composing the 5th symphony - and painting the Mona Lisa.

It is the rush of first young love and the fullness of grand parenthood. It is the thrill of victory and a gut-level understanding that all things really are possible. In short – it is being washed in the river of hope. Who wouldn't slog through hell to reach that life giving water? It is a drug. God forgive me, it is. Slurp.

Why do you think teenagers work so hard on being depressed, morose and love-less? They know what a rush they get from any relief to it. Others know that manic/depression is correlated to creativity, so in an effort to enhance their creativity they try to manufacture the illness. Sorry kids. It's a correlation, not a causation. If you make yourself mentally ill, all you get is mental illness. Creativity is gonna come on its own or not.
Same thing for all the costumes – whether goth, or freak or beatnik. The attempt to look and act creative is also vain. The truly creative, don't look "creative". In fact they look surprizingly like everyone else. Even Einstein. He always dressed in current fashion – 3-piece tweed suites while he was in Europe, heavy sweaters when he defected to American academia. His hair was the only oddity, and mostly it just looked uncombed. Other than that he looked like any other Jewish grandfather, shuffling along sucking on his pipe.

Manic/Depression, however, will get you if you have nothing to anchor yourself in the here and now of normal life. I do think that is why Franklin was so prolific in the specifics of community life: starting America's first volunteer fire department, lending library, community hospital, post office etc. Smith got his from the regimin of teaching daily classes at the university. Einstein's anchor was Mozart; a music so crisp and mathematical, that playing it reassured him that there really is a mathematical order to the universe, driven by a distinct set of dicernable rules. Luther, however, didn't have an anchor. He had forsaken the Catholic traditions, and his own theology did not spring fully formed from his head to provide an alternative. In addition, he was beset on all sides with death threats and criticism. So he latched onto his fire from God as the only thing he had to depend on. In short, he turned into a zealot. And if there is a step between that and outright paranoia it is a short one. The delusions of grandeur were simply icing on the cake. Luther was, how do I say this kindly, "troubled" by the time he died.

Variety

The Renaissance man effect may not be a cause of creativity, but it certainly seems to be a symptom. When you are in a creative high, no one task is big enough to fully occupy your mind. It has something to do with that global synergy phenomena I mentioned earlier. So at the same time that you are focusing the bulk of you energy on the primary creative task, you are also having creative eruptions on a number of different pursuits as well.

For myself, I never write one book at a time. I always have a 2nd "shadow" book in production, usually with no intention of being published. In addition, I reignite my artwork – either cartooning or photography; read anything and everything within reach, sing any and every tune in my memory banks, and beat on things with a hammer (as a cabinet maker, not axe murderer).

For many Creatives, sex is also part and parcel of the creative eruption process, usually on the edge of the perversity envelope, and certainly higher than normal in terms of frequency. Regardless of the specific activity, variety seems to nourish the Creative in several ways:

1. it bleeds off some of the adrenalin and lets you sleep

2. it clears the mind – like mental sorbet

3. it helps you feel fully alive, enmeshed in the soil

4. it heightens your creativity on the primary activity by tapping into divergent sources of ideas & energy

5. it feeds the soul.

6. if you didn't chase the variety, your head would explode.

One suspects that Washington Irving's headless horseman wasn't actually a Hessian soldier. More likely, he was a creative Dutchman who didn't have a hobby. … Pop!

13

COMMON HUMAN TOUCH
(NO MAN IS AN ATOLL; EXCEPT ON A BAD DAY)

Parents

Hans Luther, Martin's father, was a prosperous solid citizen. He was part owner of several mines and the operating partner of a major smelter, which put him squarely in the forefront of that day's high-tech industry. He was also a city councilman and a pillar of his community. So he was busy. Very, very busy. Like successful fathers of any age, he was mostly absent. Martin's mother on the other hand was from peasant stock and seemed mostly to dote on her Marty.

It's a common theme; Franklin's dad was pretty well to do himself. An entrepreneur in his own right, he squired, raised and fed 17 children, and kept his business afloat throughout all that chaos. But he was distant, which left Ben in the tender mercies of Mom, who reputedly coddled him mercilessly.

Adam Smith was the ultimate momma's boy: effete, permanently a bachelor, living under momma's roof for 57 years despite being gainfully employed.

But I like Einstein's the best. His father, Hermann Einstein, founded the electric company Elektrotechnische Fabrik J. Einstein & Cie in 1880 with his brother – a mere 6 months after Edison invented the incandescent lightbulb. He was right in the thick of things: racing for patents with the likes of Bell, Edison and Westinghouse; fighting toe-to toe with Siemans and Phillips; electrifying and lighting city after city. Hermann was an engineer by training and a salesman by temperment. He was kind, supportive, outgoing ---- and absent. Once again a prosperous but distant father.

So how was Mom? Jewish. Pauline Einstein, was the epitome of the stereotypic Jewish mother. She was doting, intrusive, demanding, meddlesome, judgemental and whiny. She disaproved of his (Albert's) 1st marriage and helped sabotage it at every turn. Then she facilitated Albert's affair with his own cousin and guided that relationship to the marriage bed. And you thought that kind of woman only existed in the back woods of Utah. Sheez.

It's as though each dad was more icon than father and each mom the first mistress. At a minimum, we can say that Dad inspired the work etheic for success and Mom provided the safety net. Both things are absolutely necessary for creativity to bloom. This is a crucial point.

- The act of crashing beyond the wall of rationality is stupendously gruesome, and very likely.
- The only ones willing to take the risk are those with nothing left to lose
- Because they are already peripheral members of society.
- BUT, they are absolutely secure and central in their families – even worshiped.
- It could just be that doting mothers are the secret ingredient of success.

Burying the old man

Each one of our guys hated what his father pushed him to do with his life. But each one loved Pop none the less and craved his acceptance and pride. So each one found a way to approach the old man's dream while charting their own course.

Hans Luther wanted Martin to be a lawyer. Martin hated law school and rejected becoming an attorney by ceremoniously dropping out of law school. But he went on to master the core of secular law – sacred law. And he argued it with the precision of a Socratic litigator.

Einstein's dad wanted him to be an engineer. The profession made his skin crawl because of its slavish dependence on math, and he abandoned it loudly. But he went on to master theoretical science, which engineers depend on daily. And ended his life as a mathematical guru.

Franklin's dad wanted him to be a printer. Ben hated printing and became a fugitive from the law in his dash for freedom. But he went on to own the printing presses in Philadelphia, and became the most successful publisher on the east coast. And publisher beats printer, every day of the week.

Smith's dad wanted him to be a merchant, something substantive, rather than being a sissy academic. He wrote Adam letter after letter on the subject, trying every trick in the book, from cajolery to threats to sanctions to bribes. It's all there in black and white. But Adam burned all his personal papers before he died. So we actually don't know. It was all just speculation on my part. So let's leave Smith out of it and speak only of the three we <u>do</u> know about. This is very interesting.

- Each of them ended up in the same basic field as Pop – despite their protests.
- Each of them did the old man one better
- Each one of them took Dad's task assignment to the abstract

As I think about this, though, I'm thinking that if it was love that pulled our geniuses into Dad's field, it wasn't their love of Dad. Afterall, note that each one of them was burying his dad in a cloud of dust. Burying. Combine that with the doting, mistress-like Moms and you'll be forced to note that Edipus is alive and well, and Mom was egging him on. Ed has not yet left the building.

Einstein seemed to have the longest, sharpest knife. His dad's whole professional life was a quest for light. The glory of light, the warmth, the speed. The … (light bulb goes on!) Aha!.
- We know where Einstein's interest in time came from.
- Maybe now we also know where his focus on the speed of light was born.

Just like in Greek mythology, the best way to kill a god is to steal his fire. And that being done, you then get to bed dear old Mom, and literally crawl back into the womb from which you came. This creativity stuff starts to take on a creepy mythic quality.

- Families are crucial to the development of Creatives
- But not in the way you'd think
- It ain't Republican family values that drive creativity

How other people affect the Creative

One of the things that struck me while researching this book is that creativity does not occur in isolation; even at the 30,000 foot level that our four geniuses traveled at. Luther was not the only one coming up with revolutionary new ideas. At the same time, Michelangelo was doing the same thing in art, while DaVinci was stirring the waters in science and engineering as well as in art. Erasmus was turning the world on its ear with his translations of the Bible, and Calvin came along to perform his own reformation of the Reformation. Machiavelli had just published <u>The Prince</u> 4 years before Luther stepped onto the world stage. It was almost as if a creative bug was abroad, infecting people simultaneously, all across Europe.

The same is true of Franklin and Smith. They didn't operate in a vacuum. Instead they were surrounded by an explosion of intellectual talent. Franklin bounced ideas off Jefferson, Madison and Monroe, the most esteemed set of next door neighbors in history. Hamilton, Adams and Paine were both a pain and a blessing. Locke and Mills contributed from a distance, and Mozart and Haydn were featured contemporary artists each evening.

Meanwhile, in the midst of haggis and heaths, Smith was part of an 80 year eruption of intellect called "The Scottish Enlightenment". It turns out that by 1776, Scotland was the best educated nation in the world, with a literacy rate of 75%, and a hot bed of new ideas in philosophy, medicine and engineering. Smith bumped into one of the other bright souls every time he turned a corner.

Yet another flowering occurs around Einstein.

- Edison, Tesla and Westinghouse were fighting it out in the electric fields;
- Karl Benz, Ransom Olds and Henry Ford were slugging their way to glory in the auto industry;
- Langley, Curtis and the Wright brothers were testing the winds in flight;
- Alexander Graham Bell was flitting all over the place dabbling in every sort of science & engineering;
- while Sigmund Freud was explaining everyone's strange yearnings for their mothers..

This distinct pattern leaves us with two lessons.

1. Creativity seems contagious, even across disciplines.

2. It also seems to run in cycles, triggered by periodic prototypes – of machines, basic technology, social systems, musical structure and what have you.

Sounding Boards

Luther, Franklin, Smith and Einstein obviously had company in the global sense. In addition, each of them also had company in his own back yard. Specifically, they each had a support group of friends, disciples and/or colleagues who served to cheer them on with unswerving devotion, as well as useful resistance and debate.

Luther had Phillip Melanchton and the boys – students and lesser faculty at Wittenberg University. Mostly they were a group of sycophants, however, Melanchton was the perfect flipside of Luther. Where Luther was brash and pompous, Melanchton was thoughtful and humble. He was the perfect foil for Luther's half-baked rages, bleeding off much of the emotion and inserting much of the theological underpinnings. In fact, he was one of the few people who could consistently weather Luther's blinding furies, by perseverance rather than strength. Without him, Luther would not have been Luther. In his own words, "I had to fight with rabble and devils, for which reason my books are very warlike. I am the rough pioneer who must break the road; but Master Phillip comes along softly and gently, sows and waters heartily,"[1]

Franklin, put together his own sounding boards. In his 20s he created "The Junto" a group of non-competing business owners and craftsmen; the movers and shakers of Philadelphia. The goal of the group was to improve the daily performance of each of them via regular group discussions on the latest business opportunities and practices, the most recent social and political issues, and developing cultural trends. In addition, they offered each other advice and counsel on the perfection of one's individual talents. A good deal of Franklin's optimism about the ability of this new species, the "Americans", to govern themselves came from this very group, as did a good deal of his comprehension of the rights of men, the role of property and the pursuit of happiness. It was his school of higher learning.

And when he had grown beyond that group, Franklin founded the American Philosophical Society, to put himself in contact with other men of continental stature and promise. They honed his thoughts as he guided them toward revolution.

Franklin's self-help peer groups survive to this day in the form of professional round table groups such as The Executive Committee (TEC), Vistage International, and The Young President's Organization (YPO), which seek to help entrepreneurs stay at the cutting edge of their professions. The uncanny thing is that these modern groups so closely resemble Franklin's groups, in structure, process and even specific discussion topics, that he could nail them on

---

[1] Martin Luther in the preface to Melanchthon's Commentary on the Colossians (1529)

intellectual property infringement, were it not for the fact that Franklin's patent and copyright protection would have expired a long time ago, and the fact that Franklin's structure, process etc. was a direct lift from the Greek symposia run by Socrates, Plato and Aristotle.

Uncertainty is, and always has been, the gravest concern for a business owner. He needs to be able to see around corners so that he can stay one step ahead of the market. He also needs to know the current "best practices". Peer groups are, and always have been the best resource on both issues.

- The Socratic Method is 3,000 years old; and it doesn't matter whether you call it peeling the onion, follow up analysis, drilling down, crawling in or hard boiled eggs. It is part of the public domain. Feel free to use it.
- The peer group model is 3,000 years old, at a minimum, and of such obvious benefit and ease of instituting that it rests in the public domain. Start one, if you can.
- One on one counseling is at least 6,000 years old, with the first formal consultation being recorded in the book of Exodus, where Laban advised Moses on how to organize a nation. Man has been seeking and giving advice and counsel since the first bar was opened.
- You can even find the specific questions to ask in the discourses of the ancient Greeks, in the works by Cicero and right there in black and white in Franklin's own guidebook for the first Junto.

Smith sat smack in the middle of a cauldron of thought, with a regular roundtable of enlightened guys that took him to task for every jot and tittle. He also had his students. And as any faculty member of standing can attest, it is impossible to be a successful lecturer and not attract a following of disciples. They are a wonderful sounding board: appreciative, supportive, even worshipful. And yet there are always a couple of students who seek to outdo each other in bringing you impressive fresh kills with which to win your favor. This usually takes the form of new knowledge, contradictory articles or books, or shrewd observations of their own. By whatever form, it all translates into the kind of safe resistance that nurtures creativity.

Einstein had the Olympia Academia, a drinking society with only 3 core members: himself and two underemployed school chums who looked to him as the best and the brightest of the misfits. These misfits, from a no-name teachers college in the Alps, of all places, were the midwives who mopped Albert's brow as he gave birth to the modern age. They did it by bringing him the latest articles and books from around the globe and arguing, caterwauling and teasing one another late into the night. They believed in him unstintingly and remained loyal to the man throughout the rest of his life. So we have another moral lesson

Creatives require a sounding board: a safe harbor where they are esteemed and loved, while being intellectually challenged.

That's why Thomas Edison, John D. Rockefeller and Harvey Firestone used to go camping together. They were a mutual admiration society, and one hell of a sounding board for each other. It's also why Mark Twain was fast friends with Nikola Tesla and a frequent fixture in his laboratory.

Competition
Competition seems to have the same impact on creativity as on any other endeavor. It brings out the best in a man. Luther was assailed on all sides. The Grand Inquisitor wanted his head, the pope, his hide. Erasmus was constantly threatening to outshine him, plus, he was beset by the worst enemies a man ever had – moralistic friends. It was impossible for Luther to take a breath without having a theological doctrine

to back it up – fully reasoned in the best Socratic method. As a result, Lutherans may have the most cohesive theological core of any branch of the Christine faith.

Franklin, of course, had the Redcoats. British troops had been an oppressive presence for 50 years, and became even worse when death warrants were issued for the rebel leaders. Nothing sharpens the senses, says the bard, like the sure knowledge of one's execution on the morrow.

Smith, on the other hand, had the odd circumstance of a competitor that wouldn't fight with him. The colonies were simply leaving the stage – one of the most powerful gestures of all time. As a result, Smith was shadow boxing, which is why his work has such an interesting quality. He had to create both sides of the argument.

Einstein, of course, had to do battle against the anti-Semites, authoritarians and traditionalists. But they were nothing compared to the impact that David Hilbert had on him. David was a disciple, literally in awe of Einstein's brilliance. As a result, Einstein's ego pushed him to spill the beans to Hilbert, about his General Theory of Relativity, and the fact that he was having trouble with the equations. Hilbert took it on himself to supply the great man with the equations that would drive the theory. In fact, he promised to send him a batch of new equations each week.

The problem was – Einstein didn't want the damn equations from Hilbert. He wanted to develop them all by himself. That way he wouldn't have to share the credit. Convinced that Hilbert was trying to steal his fire, Einstein instigated one of the all time great steeplechases of science. He scheduled a weekly seminar on his unfolding theory and ceremoniously presented a new set of equations each week to a group of awed witnesses, just prior to receiving each week's dispatch from Hilbert. Within four weeks, an exhausted Einstein had developed and presented the entire mathematical rationale for his complex theory – with David Hilbert breathing down his neck.

Immediately afterward, Einstein collapsed in nervous prostration, but secure in the knowledge that he had staved off a dastardly attack by his would be usurper. Only then, did he discover that Hilbert had no intention of taking any credit. He had only been trying to help his hero.

It seems that vanity and necessity are both the mothers of invention, which makes this politically correct in extremis.

❧

14
COMMON VALUES
(DISESTABLISHMENTARIANISM)

It is difficult to ferret out the values held in common by Creatives. They are not uniformly conservative, or liberal. They are not uniformly scientists or theologians or politicians or teachers, or engineers or mechanics or writers or musicians. They are not Christians or Muslims or Jews. They are not all Illuminati, or Freemasons (though Franklin and Smith both were). They do not even have the same obsession, although each of ours did have one.

- Luther's was the search for justification.
- Franklin's was the enjoyment of balanced hedonism.
- Smith's was a pursuit of ethics in the community.
- Einstein's was a bohemian quest for God's rulebook.

133

And then there is that one other obsession of Luther's that polite society prefers to sweep under the rug. He would have executed Einstein if given half a chance. You see, Luther was an obsessive anti-Semite and wrote the theological rationale for the eradication of the Jews, which the Nazis used 400 years later. Hitler didn't come up with the idea. Luther did. You can look it up (On the Jews and their Lies, Martin Luther, 1543). Clearly, a pure and healthy heart is not a requirement for greatness, in this or any field. I've had a lot of fun in this book at the expense of the Pope and his Catholic brethren. For the reader who has been offended, take special note. Luther was one sick puppy.

Einstein, on the other hand, evolved into an enthusiastic pacifist, socialist and Zionist. He was the instigator of the 2% movement; an attempt to get 2% of the conscripts of every nation to refuse to serve. Two percent was the magic number because that was the quantity that would cause enforcement cost to become so burdensome that regimes would collapse. He also became such a powerful icon for the Zionist movement that he was asked to serve as the President of Israel. Franklin was seriously considered for the Presidency, but he was too old and his private life made him anathema to the puritan remnant in the New England states; so Washington got the nod instead. Luther was claimed as the anti-pope by any number of peasant rebellions that sprouted across Europe in his wake. And then there was Adam Smith. Well ... nobody asked him to be anything. Oh well. It was almost a common thread. Damn.

Our four guests did not share a common definition of success, either. Luther's was based on an absolute dichotomy. Either you achieved eternal life, or you didn't. Franklin and Smith, on the other hand, both used a sliding scale of relativity. For Franklin it was balance, for Smith it was gap analysis. Oddly enough, Einstein was also an absolutist. Success was clearly defined --- complete knowledge of how everything in the universe works. There wasn't a relative bone in his body. It was a mere accident of verbiage that labeled him as the father of relativism. He had originally titled his Theory of Relativity the Theory of Variance Measurement. The fact that the beatniks took him as an icon alternately amused him and pissed him off. Isn't that a kick?

So what values <u>did</u> they share?

Anti-Authoritarianism

Luther could not abide anyone telling him what to do. If you even presumed as much he would gnaw off your arm at the elbow and force feed you the mush. He was livid at the thought of anyone exercising authority over him. If you don't grasp that one central fact, you miss the core of Luther's work. Logic was the only authority he recognized. Not mystic faith. Not titles of empire and church. Not tradition. Certainly not the point of a spear. The only authority he recognized was superior logic. And he never met anyone he felt bested him in that arena. I am sure he kept score.

Franklin, on the other hand, was a closet anti-authoritarian. Rabidly so, but in the closet. In fact, he wrote meticulous instructions for his son on how to appear to be amiably subservient while at the same time undermining the other's authority. Smith obviously bridled at the authority of both the king and the guilds, and devoted years of his life to a rationale on why both of them should willingly step into the background. And Einstein was at war with the universe. Get this. The man who was the master of time in the patent office, the tamer of time in the thought experiment, the explainer of time to the world – that same man --- was never on time. You talk about passive aggressive. See Einstein's picture in the dictionary. Let's say it loud.

You cannot be a Creative without being anti-authoritarian.

It feels good just to shout it to the roof trusses, doesn't it?

Tops and Bottoms

Creatives are Plato's boys, not Aristotle's. They start at the top with full blown theoretical outlooks and concepts and use those to reason their way horizontally, at 30,000 feet to a fully developed new theory or concept or way of life. They do not follow Aristotle's dictum. They do not start at the bottom, categorizing and counting. They don't even measure. They live in the realm of ideas, not mechanics.

Aristotle's Model	Einstein's Model
1. Record, cluster and measure everything ⇩	*1.* Don't measure, cluster or record a thing ⇩
2. Use the Socratic Method to discover prime cause ⇩	*2.* Instead, make up a very weird story. Very weird. ⇩
3. Use prime causes to develop a theory ⇩	*3.* Create a theory based on the story ⇩
4. Test the theory	*4.* Use that theory to invent more theories

Deism

There is one overriding common value that each Creative seems to have. In one form or another they are all Deists. There are lots of variations within Deism, but there is a dicernible common core. Deists believe there is a supreme being. They believe he created this world, and then left it to run as a self-sustaining operation, based on unchangeable natural laws. He is now absent or at least distant, and does not hover over us keeping score. Nor does he whisper words of revelation in a prophet's ear or perform miracles.

I knew that Franklin and Smith were both avowed and publicly recognized Deists. I learned that the same was true of Einstein. But Luther was the one that had me stumped. How in the world could a theologian, obsessed with salvation and eternal life, be a Deist? Then it struck me. Of course he was a Deist! Look at his approach.

- It was a quest for the unchanging natrual laws of God
- It was fueled and directed by logic, not by mysticism
- It relied on a covenant, not a whim
- It was a contract which God offered to Man – from the beginning of time
- All man had to do was say Yes. Everything else followed automatically. No further action by God.
- Bing, bang, boom. It's Deism with a twist. The gospel of grace made it a contract.

Once I recognized that, everything fell into place for me. Of course you have to be a Deist to be a Creative. Everything we do, most especially at the theoretic and strategic level, is tied directly or indirectly to the dominant faith of our culture. In our case it's the Judeo-Christian faith. In the Middle East it's Islam, and so forth across the globe. Now look back at the story laid out in this chapter and you will see that it doesn't matter what the discipline – religion, politics, economics, science, you name it – every Creative is searching for the basic natural law that governs their corner of the universe. But to get to that natural law, you have to <u>believe</u> in natural law, and that means you need to get beyond your own god.

You must move beyond the image of an activist, personal god that the religions of the world cling to for both spiritual comfort and temporal power.

Then and only then does the wall become passable. Up until then, you are simply bashing yourself against the rampart. You will never get out into the meadow.

> *(AUTHOR'S NOTE: I don't really like what I just said. It offends my fundamentalist sensibilites. It seems sacreligious. It goes against so much of what I was taught to believe. Heck, it goes against so much of what I have believed on my own volition for my entire adult life. This is crazy. I have just given myself a paradigm shift. I don't know whether I am approaching something or whether it's all rushing down on me. As I write this, it makes me dizzy. Not yet nauseous, but that will probably come. I will sign off for now and come back to this when things settle down a bit.*
>
> *(AUTHOR'S 2nd NOTE: Okay. A week has now passed. I'm back.)*

So, what have we learned?
Jason Bracklwhythe lived right down the street from Ben Franklin as a boy. They played together, went to church together were apprenticed together and ran away from their apprenticeships at the same time. Jason lived in the same world of supermen as Ben, but Jason ended up cleaning his toenails every night rather than doing anything interesting with his life. Why is that? Because nothing in this chapter will make you creative. Let me repeat something I said earlier.

"… environment affects Creatives. It determines, in part, who they become, what they see, how they work, what they value and the risks they are willing to take."

I still stick by that comment. It is obviously true. But it is just as obviously incomplete. So let me add a trailer to it.

"…are willing to take. **But the creativity, itself --- the insight, the logic, the 'magic' --- comes from something else. The most that others can do is mold, direct or influence the focus and method of a Creative. They have no control over the creativity itself".**

But, just so you have a tool for your own work on the subject. Let me offer the scoreboard we've constructed. These are the things that Creatives have in common.

	External	Internal
Impersonal	• Power Balance • Safety vs control • Inclusion/exclusion • Access to knowledge • SpaceTime • Vocation	• The Id • The Ego • The SuperEgo • Manic/depression • Theoretic frame • Deism
Personal	• Creative clusters • Sounding Boards • Competition	• Edipal obsessions • Anti-authoritarian • Necessity • Vanity

15

EGO, FAITH & RISK
(THE METAPHYSICS OF CREATIVITY)

Science works best when we have issues that can be broken down into simple physical functions with a very limited number of variables. When the issue is a complex array of inseparable functions with an infinite number of variables, however, science falters. And in its place, we are forced to use metaphysical disciples such as philosophy, theology, psychology and a host of other "-ologies". That is the case with creativity. It is too complex to map scientifically. So we must part company with Aristotle at this point. If you're not willing to engage in "mushy thinking" you haven't got a chance, because - - -

Art kick-starts Science.

I would like to live in a mountain hermitage, something with a wide wrap-around veranda. I'd also like to let my beard grow to preposterous proportions. Something along the line of ZZ Top. Those things would lend credence to my words when you crested the summit and asked me what drives creativity. I would stroke my luxuriant growth and gaze into the far distance, then with a twinkle in my eye I'd lean way over and softly ask you three questions.

1. Who helped Ludwig?

2. Why is mustard key?

3. When did Orville become a lynchpin?"

Gurus always answer questions with questions. It's an annoying tick we've got and I apologize profusely for it but there you have it. Creativity rests on a three-legged stool, of ego, faith and risk. They are the components, the very pieces parts of the engine that drives a Creative on his quest.

Who Helped Ludwig?

It may take a village to raise a child, but Ludwig von Beethoven worked alone. He may have had the tunes and philosophies of every prior composer swimming in his head while he worked, He may have had the voice of Joseph Haydn, his mentor, humming in his ears, but his 5th Symphony was a thing itself --- the singular, definitive bridge that confiscated the baton from the metronome and gave it to the heart. Beethoven invented soul long before Detroit found natural rhythm. Go listen to a little Haydn, and as icing on the cake, serve yourself a bit of Mozart. I'll wait.

Go ahead. I really will wait.

Hayden -
http://www.youtube.com/watch?v=lLjwkamp3lI&feature=related

Mozart –
http://www.youtube.com/watch?v=Qb_jQBgzU-I

You have just sampled some of the world's most glorious
classic music. Pristine. Mathematical in its precision.
Predictable. All working off the same handbook to the secrets
of the universe. When you listen to classical music you know
that God's in his heaven and all's right with the world.

Now – listen to Beethoven's 5th Symphony. Close your eyes,
and turn up the volume.   I'll wait.

http://www.youtube.com/watch?v=B7pQytF2nak&feature=related

Now, listen to Beethoven's "Ode to Joy" ---- and if you leave
the volume up, just fasten your seatbelt.

http://www.youtube.com/watch?v=M-
WF0PVi2FA&feature=related

God ain't in heaven anymore, is he?. He's in your underwear
drawer, and he's gettin' busy. This was a new sound – one
that had never been heard before – and has rarely been
duplicated since. It is the sound of the primal beast in full
fury. It is passion and carnage. It prowls across the mind in
fits and starts and grabs the soul by its short hairs. A
committee would have smoothed it out. A work group would
have used the procedure manual to figure a way back to the
metronome. A wife would certainly have knocked off a few
rough edges and made it less, you know, rude. But this baby
was Ludwig's – all by himself. Who helped Ludwig?
Nobody! He did it by himself.

The Role of the Individual

It is physically impossible for more than one person to have a specific new idea at the same time. It can't be done. You can lock them in a room for two days and the best you'll get is a joyous, rapid fire brain storm where each individual contributes a tiny piece to the puzzle, stepping on the idea of the prior guy and getting stepped on by the next guy in line. But the fact remains that

each individual idea
comes out of the mind
of a single individual.

And some ideas are just better than others. I subscribe to Henry Luce's "Great Man" Theory. Luce was the founder of TIME magazine and a strong believer that individuals shape history. That's why TIME has a "Man of the Year" cover story each year (now stretched by political correctness to be person- people-computer-planet etc of the year) dedicated to the one person who had the biggest impact on the world during the previous 12 months. Adolph Hitler has graced that cover, as has Joseph Stalin, the Ayatollah Khomeini, Albert Einstein and Mahatma Gandhi. The award is not given to the nicest guy. It's given to the guy who had the single biggest individual impact on the globe during the prior year. TIME even devoted a cover story to the person of the *century*. Einstein won that honor as well.

As soon as you finish this book, I think there's one more you should read – Ayn Rand's Atlas Shrugged. It will keep you awake at night as you discover who John Galt is. Actually it'll keep you awake for lots of nights – it's over 1,000 pages long (unless you get a version with readable sized type – then it's 5,000 pages long.) I think Ayn had it right - gifted individuals are the well spring of society.

Then what about the Sounding Board?

They're a group, after all. And I've made a pretty strong case for them being integral to the creative process. So what gives? That's a stumper, until you ponder it for a moment. The sounding board is there as an audience. They are <u>not</u> main actors in the drama. They are not equals. They are reactive, not proactive. In fact, if they start to be proactive, they are shown the door. That's what happened to Carl Jung. He started out as one of Sigmund Freud's groupies. But then Jung started to think for himself and he and Freud split, with enough antipathy to doom the relationship. The same was also true of Plato and Aristotle. When Aristotle left the conceptual plain and started to measure and categorize everything, Plato dismissed him as a toolie, and never sent him another Christmas card. And that, ladies and gentlemen, is a fact. Not one Christmas card has ever been found.

The Sounding Board is there to be a sounding board. Mostly inert. Always in awe. Occasionally curious. It's first job is to provide a safe harbor for the Creative's ego. Second, they are to help him by getting him to talk out load. Ideas never fully gel until we have to express them to someone. Third, they are to feed him the latest in cutting edge knowledge, like little magpie gossips ("You wouldn't believe what Mr Somebody over at XYZ is about to announce ...". "Look at what the <u>Wall Street Journal</u> said yesterday".). And finally, they are occasionally allowed to ask "Are you sure?". The rest of the load is carried by the Creative.

Why is the Individual Key?

Only one person in the history of the globe has the unique combination of talents, genetics, aptitudes, personality, knowledge, beliefs, experience etc. etc. etc. etc. that combine to unlock the secret of (you fill in the blank). The simple fact of the matter is a straight forward mathematical one. The individual is the only entity complex enough to synthesize all the necessary variables into a cohesive whole. Groups can't generate, or handle, that level of complexity. That's because a group has an ulterior motive. It has to function as a single entity. It has to agree on something, or perform a task, or simply get along well enough so that nobody gets killed. Any of those agendas cause the group to simplify, simplify – because the fewer issues they confront, the fewer points of contention there will be. So individuals are always more complex than groups.

My father tried out for the varsity basketball team 5 times – on 5 successive days – each time using a different name. He didn't know how to quit, and he certainly never gave up. My mother condemned her own father to death, because there were other people in the hospital who needed the blood that would have been given to him. At that time, doctors didn't know how to cure Grandy, whereas the other 2 people were accident victims who could definitely be saved. She told Grandy as much, then held him in her arms while he bled to death. That's what you call steely resolve. I was raised by those two people. You think those characteristics made their way into me, either by blood or by training? Of course they did. But I've never once shared that information with a group. It's none of their damn business. It would also be counter productive – because neither trait is useful, or valued, within a group. They do not lend themselves to self-effacing compromise or tolerance for pessimism in others. I may not even have told my wife. Same reason.

So why do I share it now? Because this book is a solo project. It is all mine. It sinks or swims on me. My talent. My experience. My insights. My ability to string nouns and verbs together into some kind of meaningful message. Me me me mememememe. And that makes those bits of individual background extremely important, and useful. Because steely resolve and tenacity are crucial in the pursuit of creativity --- at least as I see it.

EGO

You cannot breech the Wall of Rationality without an ego the size of Texas. I could meticulously run the list of our four guests, and of the eight people before them and the 16 before that and so on, all the way back to Socrates. But by this point you'll just have to take my word for it – or go do the research yourself. It slows down the narrative to do that kind of thing. So let's agree to the ego assertion and move on to the more interesting issue --- why do you need a big ego?

1. By definition, the Wall of Rationality defines what is rational. Anything which occurs within it is rational. Anything that occurs outside it is irrational and therefore dangerous. Anything creative exists outside the current Wall and is therefore irrational and dangerous. You have to have a big ego just to have something to stand on so you can see over the wall, where the new ideas live. Without the ego, you won't have even a seed of an idea.

2. And that ego pales in comparison to the one that allows you to actually go beyond the wall yourself and actively play out in the meadow where the wild things grow. Your ego has to believe that you can outrun, out think, out muscle whatever exists out there that scares everyone else so much. Otherwise you will never develop the seed into a full blown idea.

3. The universal "I". Einstein's rule of thumb for evaluating any hypothesis, premise or theory was to ask himself, "If I were God, would I have created the world to operate this way?" That's a pretty heady approach to life, but it is, in point of fact, roundly shared if not as openly admitted by other Creatives as well. If I'm the only one willing to step outside the wall, I have no other benchmark against which to compare my thoughts and actions.

4. Unless he has his head in the sand, every Creative knows that he is different. He gets things that others don't. He

sees things that they miss. He becomes acutely aware that he has talents that others don't. You can dress it up anyway you want, but when you've spent a lifetime knowing you are special, a certain sense of self confidence goes with it.

5. The final reason for ego is that you're all you have. Other folks may very well reject you. Friends may very well turn against you. Ultimately, no one else will quite get it, since by definition, you're different. And be guaranteed, no one else will go over the wall with you at first. So when you're all you have, you tend to over estimate the strength, wisdom and goodness of the only lifeline you've got. Hope springs eternal.

Some Creatives wear their ego on their sleeve. They are obnoxious or condescending, demanding or judgmental. Others, however, are the epitome of humility. They "hazard a guess" instead of making a pronouncement. They do an "aw shucks" self denigration, for public consumption. They pull a Michelangelo. When the world's greatest sculptor was complemented he would retort, "all I did was get the gravel out of the way."

Ego plays itself out in those drastically different ways due to a phenomena known as the equity effect. Humans constantly compare themselves to others. It's a disease we have. And if we run out of people to compare ourselves to we invent an ideal self against which to compare. Am I as tall, thin, good looking, rich, smart, popular, happy etc., etc., ad infinitum.

And anytime I am different, I have to be able to give myself a reason.

> I'm not as rich as I ought to be (or as my neighbor is) because … I know, because my old man wasted his time

trying out for stupid basketball teams rather than being a bank president.

Or –

I'm richer than I ought to be (or --- than my neighbor is) because I happened to guess right on that land deal 20 years ago.

If there is a clear and obvious reason, one that makes sense to me, then life is fair and balanced (ie – there is equity) and I can go about my business. But when there isn't an obvious reason, I'll have to make one up, or I won't be able to relax. So what happens when you consistently notice that you are creative when others are not?

- If you demand to see yourself as normal, then the reason can only be that other people are less than normal – ie. there's something wrong with them.

- And since there's nothing visibly wrong with them, they're probably lazy as well as stupid, because anyone could have figured this out if they'd just tried.

- You will therefore treat them as the pond scum they are and all will be right with the world.

Oddly enough, the Creatives who see themselves as ordinary are the most likely to be the obnoxious egotists. The Creatives who acknowledge their uniqueness, however, are the most likely to be gracious and easy on the nerves. They know there's nothing wrong with the other folks.

But is ego all there is?

Mustard and Poetry (sometimes the two **can** mix)

"If you can keep your head when all about you
Are losing theirs and blaming it on you,
If you can trust yourself when all men doubt you
But make allowance for their doubting too,
If you can wait and not be tired by waiting,
Or being lied about, don't deal in lies,
Or being hated, don't give way to hating,
And yet don't look too good, nor talk too wise:
If you can dream--and not make dreams your master,
If you can think--and not make thoughts your aim;
If you can meet with Triumph and Disaster
And treat those two impostors just the same;
If you can bear to hear the truth you've spoken
Twisted by knaves to make a trap for fools,
Or watch the things you gave your life to, broken,
And stoop and build 'em up with worn-out tools:
If you can make one heap of all your winnings
And risk it all on one turn of pitch-and-toss,
And lose, and start again at your beginnings
And never breathe a word about your loss;
If you can force your heart and nerve and sinew
To serve your turn long after they are gone,
And so hold on when there is nothing in you
Except the Will which says to them: "Hold on!"
If you can talk with crowds and keep your virtue,
Or walk with kings--nor lose the common touch,
If neither foes nor loving friends can hurt you;
If all men count with you, but none too much,
If you can fill the unforgiving minute
With sixty seconds' worth of distance run,
Yours is the Earth and everything that's in it,
And--which is more--you'll be a Man, my son!"

"IF", by Rudyard Kipling 1910

Kipling is obviously talking about something more than ego. He's talking about faith. Before you even begin, you better believe that you can do it. Otherwise, you will falter soon after leaving the starting blocks. It just takes too much work, at too big a risk – unless you have faith. Jesus said "If you have even the faith of a mustard seed, you can move mountains." Have you ever seen a mustard seed? It is a tiny, tiny thing, just about this (→ •) size. Now that's not much. So my question to you is, "Would you like a second seed?"

FAITH

Einstein constantly referred to God. Franklin preferred the term divine providence. Smith, being a proper Scot, was a familiar of God Almighty. And Luther, of course, fought as much with God as he did with everybody else. Faith is crucial to creativity on several levels, however, the crucial faith is NOT faith in God.

First, Creatives have faith in the existence of natural law. Our investigation found that this took place in the context of Judeo-Christian Deism. But our investigation was blatantly biased. I only chose people well known in Western culture. I will guarantee you that there is a strain of deism that runs through every religion, whether it be Islam, Buddhism, Hinduism, Zoroastrianism or any other ism. And those believers in natural law are, will be, and have been, the source of creativity. Yaweh does not have a monopoly on creative juices. Nor does any deity. Therefore, let me be so bold as to suggest that it is faith in the natural law itself, not in the deity who may or may not have established it, which seems to nurture creativity. And that is why an atheist can be just as creative as a Baptist.

Second, Creatives have faith in themselves. We brushed against this topic while discussing Ego. But what, exactly, is it about themselves that Creatives have faith in? That's an easy one. The answer is --- Competence. Creatives believe

150

they will succeed. They stand there on the precipice, prepared to vault beyond the wall, where nothing but uncertainty, failure and shame are reputed to exist. And yet they have a little distracted grin on their face, because they know down in their gut that they are going to bring back a victory. Take a look at every statue, bust and painting of Ben Franklin. He looks like the Mona Lisa in every single one of them. It's that enigmatic smile. He knows something that you don't. Always did. Always will. Same thing goes for Einstein. Even Smith had it. Luther had it too, but only after a couple tankards of beer. When sober, he was dealing with too many other demons. But he, like the others, was always supremely self confident. But confident about what, exactly ?

- **Endurance** – Creatives know they can outlast a mule. Eighteen hour days are nothing when they're fully engaged.
- **Intensity** – Creatives can focus. They can peel wallpaper with the heat they generate.
- **Solution finding** - Problem solving is for amateurs. Creatives invent solutions.
- **The compass in their nose** – They know where "intellectual north" is, at all times, so they always have a sense of direction in their quest.
- **Insight** – You and I see a traffic jam. The Creative sees a tear in the social fabric, which disrupts families and marriages by requiring that people travel to a central location to transact business. So instead of building more highways, he invents the internet.

Third, Creatives have faith in "The Gift" – somebody gave the Creative a special gift. Nobody knows why, not even the Creative himself. It's like large breasts, good looks and athletic ability.   It just happens. He certainly didn't do anything to deserve it. It just showed up. And he knows that it could all go away tomorrow - for no reason whatsoever. But while he's got it he knows he's got it.   And he relies on it regularly. And that is what faith in your own competence looks like.

Fourth, Creatives have faith in "the call". They know they are the one. They often don't know <u>which</u> one, but they know they are <u>the</u> one. There is some crucial task that needs to be performed, or some great mystery which needs to be solved, and the Creative takes it on, not because of the importance of the task or mystery but because it is a vehicle for discovering a new part of the natural law. The current world, the concrete world in which you and I live, lacks substance to a Creative. It's not exactly transparent to them, but it is an awful lot like gossamer, like a sheer curtain that prevents clarity, but provides strong visual cues as to what lies beyond. And the Creative is acutely aware of being called by something or someone to go beyond that veil.

Fifth, Creatives have faith in the benevolence of the world. If they bear down, focus, put in the hours, and give vent to the full array of their intellectual gifts --- they really and truly believe that everything will work out. It will work out because they are questing after natural law, which is absolutely rational, absolutely integrated, absolutely useful to know. It will work out because people are generally rational and kind hearted, and they will eventually come around. Just wait. You'll see.

But what if ... ?

The Apostle Paul defined faith as hope in the unseen, the untouchable, the unmeasurable. He, therefore, was placing his own work in direct opposition to Aristotle's, who said you had to be able to see it, touch it, measure it and categorize it for there to be any substance to what ever you were considering. Of course, Aristotle was talking about knowledge – not about faith. And therein lies the rub. You see ...

the logical pursuit of Natural Law depends on the mysticism of faith

I <u>don't</u> know for a fact that I will be able to summon the endurance, intensity, insight etc. one more time. I don't know for a fact that natural law even exists, or that everything will actually work out ok. I just hope that all of that comes to be. That's faith.

- But what if none of it is true?
- What if there really isn't a Natural Law underlying all of life?
- What if I'm <u>not</u> crucial to uncovering bits and pieces of it?
- What if I <u>am</u>, but I lack the skill, endurance, focus etc.?
- Or what if the Grand Inquisitor will strap me to a stake the moment he learns what I'm trying to do?

Then all that faith of mine is for naught.
Then what in the hell do I do?

COURAGE

Orville became the lynchpin when he climbed into the contraption on that fateful day at Kittyhawk, North Carolina. We're on our way to Mars because Orville Wright had the courage to fly that first airplane 200 feet. If creativity were easy, everyone would do it. But it's dangerous work. You can lose your health, wealth, marriage, sanity and friends. Not to mention, your good name. All for simply stepping beyond the wall. Sometimes, just for peeking over the wall. For that simple reason, courage may be the single most important element of creativity. The willingness to think beyond the wall.

Peeking over the wall is the easy part. But that's not much good unless you act on what you see, and that's where many people fall by the wayside. It takes courage to vault the wall, because what you discover on the other side of the wall might just eat you alive. Even when it's tame, it's still unfamiliar and easily rejected. So sometimes the scariest part is simply raising your hand and saying "I have an idea."

Ron Lee, Lutheran cleric and researcher on creativity reinforces this with his findings on the importance of stubbornness in creativity. He's found that the most creative leaders are downright pigheaded. When you have the courage to chase your vision, nothing can stop you. Nothing. Death may slow you down a bit, but nothing permanently stops you.

The institution of civil rights - for blacks and women - was an act of creativity. Someone had to see beyond the so-called "natural" law, that both were chattel property. But unless someone had also acted on that vision, and kept acting on it – again and again and again and again - blacks and women would still be locked in their old roles even to this day. If you doubt that, just take a look at the Muslim fundamentalists. Those folks have not gotten beyond one of those walls quite yet.

Action is what brings creativity to fruition.
It also brings the wrath of Khan down upon you. Just ask Martin Luther King. No, wait. You can't. He was assassinated. Neither can you ask Gandhi, nor Malcolm X, nor Bobby Kennedy. Same reason. It seems that anyone who imagines a world different than the current one is always eliminated; or laughed at in class, or passed over for promotions at work. As I said earlier – creativity is not safe.

That's why courage is so important. And that's why it is the substance desperately sought by the cowardly lion in The Wizard of Oz ... and a good many executives as well.

154

What makes a King out of a slave? Courage!
What makes the flag on the mast to wave? Courage!
What makes the elephant charge his tusk
in the misty mist, or the dusky dusk?
What makes the muskrat guard his musk? Courage!
What makes the Sphinx the Seventh Wonder?
Courage!
What makes the dawn come up like thunder?
Courage!

What makes the Hottentot so hot?
What puts the ape in ape-ricot?
What have they got [I wish I'd] got?
Courage.[2]

Talent is far less important than courage.

So stop worrying about how "good" you are. Instead, if you really have to worry about something, worry about how brave you are. Because without the courage to look, you'll never see a new idea. Without the courage to act, your idea will simply evaporate in the ether, unseen and unheard by any, save the cobwebs of your own mind. Without courage you will second-guess yourself into an early grave, without ever actually doing something worthwhile. As the classics tell us ...

The coward dies a thousand deaths.
The valiant dies but once.

So zip up your equipment and arm yourself with what Descartes **should** have said,

I think, therefore I do.

Getting a handle on Courage

Risk is the probability that something negative will happen to us as a result of our own actions, such as … what's the likelihood I'll get berated for suggesting that we paint the stadium bright pink? Better still, what's the likelihood of losing my membership at the athletic club for suggesting that women might not be chattel property?

It might help you understand your own capacity for courage if we look at it from two perspectives: (a) the degree of risk, and (b) the location of risk.

The degree of risk. If I get fined $10 for doing a thing, I may be willing to do it again and again, because $10 is just $10. However, if I spend 7 years in jail for the same action, that would probably have a chilling effect on my willingness to do that action again. It doesn't take much courage to risk a $10 fine. It takes considerably more to risk 7 years in the slammer. Courage is the willingness to sustain a creative quest in spite of considerable personal cost.

The location of Risk. There are two types of risk - Challenges and Threats. Threats are the potential bad things that will attack me from inside my safe harbor: my physical safety, my paycheck, my security, my reputation, my love life, etc. Challenges, on the other hand, are the potential bad things that take place outside of my safe harbor: a downturn in the Iranian economy, the termination of an unknown vice president of some nameless company, the inability to dry up a zit on some teenager's face. Threats cause me to stress out and short circuit, but I can live with challenges all day long. In fact challenges (safe risks) invigorate me. So as long as I assume that the unknown is a challenge, I have the heart of a lion. The real kind.

And what, pray tell, keeps courage burning?
Courage depends on the unholy assumptions of Ego, Faith and Risk. Unholy, not because of any lack of virtue, but simply because I don't want to over-claim or over-promise.

EGO – the assumption that I am central to the universe (at this moment in time, I am the one in a position to act).

FAITH – assumptions about myself- fluctuating from "I think I'm up to the task" to "I am the Lord's anointed." Assumptions about the ultimate benevolence of the world (if I try really hard, things will work out). Assumptions about others (if I just hang in there, others will catch on or buy in etc).

RISK - assumptions about the degree and location of risk.

And then there's Luck
I've spent the past 20 years of my life as a Vistage Chair. I mentioned Vistage earlier (It used to be called TEC --- The Executive Committee). It is one of the peer groups that has grown out of Franklin's Junto, and Socrates' school. Grown to 20,000 members worldwide. But so little has changed from what they did, they'd feel right at home at one of our meetings. The folks I deal with there are exclusively entrepreneurs; the folks who mortgage the farm (or house) to start their own business. And the thing that strikes me – and it doesn't matter whether they're doing $3 million a year or $8 Billion – is that they all attribute their continued existence to hard work and LUCK. Not to brilliance. They just have to stay on their feet and work like a dog, and the god's of fortune will somehow smile on them at the 11th hour. And more often than not, they do. It's the damnedest thing. As a result, one of the ways they monitor each other's welfare is to ask, "Are you feeling lucky, yet?"

Here's the point

Courage depends completely on how you interpret your life. So learn to interpret it boldly.

- You betcha I'm up to the task.
- I can outlast, outfight, out think out-everything everyone.
- Besides, it'll all work out in the end.
- And even if it doesn't, what's the worst that could happen?
- I mean, really.
- Besides, if I just catch a little luck, it'll work.

In short, you play a head game on yourself. That's how you bolster courage. Come to think of it, faith is a head game too. Hmmm, what do you know? So is Ego.

Could it be that the secret to creativity is what we tell ourselves …

- about ourselves, and
- about the world in which we live?

End Note

Source: The Wizard of OZ, Universal Studios as quoted at http://www.filmsite.org/wiza3.html

You might want to look at Viktor Frankel's Man's Search for Meaning to answer that last question

158

… or …
is it based on
what we <u>do</u>
?

16

DOING CREATIVITY IN THE CLOUDS
(PROCESS ON THE MOUNTAIN TOP)

To understand how you actually <u>do</u> creativity on the mountain top, we need to bring one more guest to our table – Henry Ford. True, he never took on the pope, or the king. Neither did he establish a new international political economy nor define the laws of nature. But he did put America on wheels, and thereby changed the way we work, play and think. Let's take a look.

Henry did not invent the automobile.[1] . He simply redefined it's use. Before he hit the scene, automobiles were considered novelty items, expensive toys for the rich - so they were put together by small teams of craftsmen who handled the whole process, from axel construction to seat cushion installation.

Ford decided the automobile could be an everyday necessity for every man, no matter how rich or poor - and he turned to mass production technology in order to make it cheap enough for every Tom, Dick and Harry to afford it. But he still had a problem. The common man could afford it - but he couldn't use the darn thing, because most of the nation's roads were still dirt or gravel tracks that turned into hopeless mud holes. So he was in the same position as daVinci 400 years prior. Ford had an idea that was ahead of his time. SO --- he had a decision to make. He could decide that it was a bad idea and kill it, or, he could damn the torpedoes and sail full speed ahead. Get the picture; there's Ford, a couple hundred thousand in debt, with a wife and family looking pie-eyed and a mother-in-law muttering "I told you he was no good." But instead of shutting it down and getting a good steady job as a farm mechanic, Ford decided to pull a Noah.

The similarities were uncanny. Ford had a car, but no roads. Noah had a boat, a big boat, a big 〰️🔴⚜️#♞★ boat, but no water. Except for being completely different, they were exactly the same. There's a lesson in there about where to look for inspiration. There's also a lesson here about how far to carry an analogy, because Noah was on good terms with the Almighty. All he had to do was issue raincoats and grab a lawn chair. Ford, however, was on his own.

So he did the same thing that Luther, Franklin, Smith and Einstein did. He kept plugging right along like a stubborn mule, because he knew that he was strong enough, and clever enough and lucky enough to figure things out. And he knew that things would work out, because it was time. The car was an idea whose time had come. And he wasn't quitting, no matter what his wife, mother-in-law or bank did. That's courage in the trenches.

But there are a lot of dead soldiers with courage. The trick is to be one of the live ones at the end of the day. For that you need a plan.

Reality is a Bummer

The best laid plans of mice and men often go awry, precisely when they bump into harsh reality. I'd like to flap my arms and fly, but gravity prevents it. I'd like to wish myself to Hawaii every Friday afternoon, but the physical laws of matter prevent it. Ford wanted to sell a vast number of cars, but the lack of paved roads prevented it.

The world around us imposes limits on creativity; and most people are tempted to react with a shrug, a murmured "Oh Well" and a return to the safety of the tried and true. That reaction allows them to sleep the stress-free slumber of the noble victim, but it doesn't do squat for the welfare of humanity or their own personal fortunes. The academic term for such actions is "half-assed creativity". One bun may be hanging over the meadow, but the other bun sits firmly atop the wall of rationality, gripping the bricks so that retreat is easy and painless.

It would be nice if a more genteel name could be found for the phenomena, but accuracy sometimes demands rough language. Anyway, Ford had a problem. He'd sunk so much money into the project - and run so far out into the meadow - that both buns were impossibly far from the wall. He couldn't get back inside the wall unless he declared bankruptcy. As a result, he had to do something about the reality he faced, or he would have gone under.

Coping With Reality

What can you do with reality? You can embrace it as it is. You can step back from it and try to isolate yourself from it. Or you can stand your ground and contend with it, trying to generate a little change. And you can do any of these actively or passively.

FIGURE 16-1: Coping with Reality

	CONTEND	EMBRACE	WITHDRAW
ACTIVE	Change it - substance - image	Take charge of existing reality	Create or find new reality
PASSIVE	Adapt to it	Join the existing reality	Become a wall-flower

Ford's competition offered only 6 inches of clearance, from ground to running board. Ford responded to the road conditions by raising the chassis high enough to clear the average rut in a dirt road. That one change moved a lot of cars. But not nearly enough to clear out his enormous inventory. That's because he didn't solve the problem. In order to be practical, cars required a network of paved roads. Duh. His innovation was simply a passive attempt to contend with the world via adaptation. So, while he was exceedingly clever, he was still just a clever failure. Can you imagine the frustration? Just imagine this was your life. You've been brilliant, twice.

1. You perfected mass production for a new and terribly complex product, then ran smack into the wall of reality. The average rut is deeper than 5 inches.

2. So you got brilliant again, you raise the chassis, only to find that it only got you part way up the wall ... which simply wasn't good enough. You needed something that didn't even exist --- a highway system. A friggin' highway system. Not even governments could afford that.

We all buy the old cliché, "If at first you don't succeed, try, try again." But if at <u>second</u> you don't succeed, shouldn't you simply smarten up and quit?

But Ford was a stubborn S.O.B., not to mention a desperate one. He was also wonderfully insightful, and he remembered something that most of us forget in moments of despair - reality is moveable. After all, the reality was that cars didn't even exist ... up until Karl-Friedrich Benz made the first one in 1885. So Ford expanded the reasoning --- paved roads didn't exist, but they *could*.

Through that simple observation, Henry Ford took a mammoth step. He moved from passively adapting to reality, to actively changing it. Take another look at Figure 1 and you'll see that that's just one little step for a man, but one giant step for mankind (and a borrowed cliché to boot).

Changing Reality

Like Noah, Henry Ford beseeched the Lord for paved roads, and God provided. On the morning of November 3rd, 1914, America awoke to the complete interstate road system we know today. It had dropped from heaven like manna.

Wouldn't that be nice? The problem is that Noah's tactic doesn't usually work for the rest of us. So in the absence of deus ex machina (intervention from heaven) we are left to contend with reality on our own. And sometimes, the only way to change one aspect of reality is to embrace another aspect of reality. In Henry's case that other reality was money.

He knew that Alexander Graham Bell and Thomas Edison had both faced the exact same problem - marvelous inventions that no one could use until the means to use them were in place. So Bell and Edison had done the logical thing. They ran wires across town and across the nation. They had joined the existing reality pioneered by telegraph wiring, poured money into it, and reaped the rewards.

There was only one problem that Henry could see. Edison and Bell had been foolish. They'd invested their own money up front and waited 40 years to recoup the investment. That may have been okay if all you were running was one skinny little wire. But the cost of paving just one mile of road could finance 793 miles of electric or phone cable - and Henry just didn't have that kind of dough, and couldn't possibly beg, borrow or steel it. So joining the existing reality was out of the question. Boom! That's the third wall in a row to smash Ford in the face.

Controlling Reality

Three strikes and you're out. Maybe. Another option is that after the third strike you change the rules of the game. And that's just what Ford did. He decided he'd do some creative double dipping.

He'd get Americans to pay twice for his cars. First, he'd get them to pay for paving the roads out of their own pockets, whether they used the roads or not. Then he'd get them to pay a second time, this time for the cars they'd just made feasible by their previous largess. But that was a pretty tall order, since American's had spent 20 years consistently voting down just about every bond issue or tax increase that had to do with paving roads. Americans clearly didn't want paved roads. They were too expensive. Boom! A forth strike. But at this point Henry no longer cared. He'd already changed the rules.

He sent a troop of public relations men to every corner of the nation, armed with the new-fangled slide projector, a script and a megaphone. Their message in every city and hamlet was vintage apple pie and corn bread, with the emphasis on corn. No mention was ever made that Ford stood to benefit from paved roads. No mention was ever made of the cost. Instead, the message focused on empire and greatness.

Greatness was a hot topic because of Teddy Roosevelt's recent successes in imperialism. There was a sense that the U.S. was about to join the short list of great nations and folks were looking for that last factor that would push them over the top.

Ford supplied it. Paved roads. "Look at the Romans," his men said. "What did they have that set them apart? The Apian Way and a full network of paved roads that connected a far flung empire ... and helped hold it together." A little patriotic background music. A couple shots of the flag unfurled along a glorious highway. "Roads, my friend. I said Paved Roads. Right here in River City." The Music Man had the decided hum of a carburetor.

Congress was besieged by a populace demanding the very roads they'd been rejecting for two decades. Almost immediately, America embarked on a massive road building campaign, and then consumers bought Ford's cars in droves. He was making money hand over fist and Americans had been suckered into paying twice for the privilege of driving.

That was the crowning glory of Henry Ford's career.
- He didn't invent the car, Karl Benz did.
- He didn't pioneer mass production. Eli Whitney did that, back in the 1700's.
- He didn't even invent paved roads. The Romans did that back in 200 B.C.

What he did do, and it remains to his everlasting credit, was to build a new wall out in the meadow. The old wall that surrounded the concept of roads was made from the bricks of economics --- "we can't afford to have them". Ford vaulted that wall and built a new one, way out in the meadow, made with the bricks of empire and glory --- "we can't afford not to have roads".

He redefined reality.
The rest was easy.

Ford and Full-Fanny Creativity

You may have noticed that Henry Ford is a painless teaching tool. In the process of narrating his efforts we've just walked through the entire coping matrix in Figure 1, because Ford tried every single compartment, except being a wall-flower (see Figure 2).

FIGURE 16-2

	CONTEND	EMBRACE	WITHDRAW
ACTIVE	*Change reality* Pave the roads	*Control reality* Change their minds	*Create Reality* Re-define roads
PASSIVE	*Adaptation* Create more Clearance	*Join reality* Use corporate tools	*Exit reality* Go belly up

• He tried adaptation via a raised running board
• He wanted to change reality by building roads
• To do so he had to join the existing realities in engineering and finance
• He controlled reality by changing people's minds
• And he did that by creating a new reality, one in which the world was viewed in terms of empire and glory instead dollars and cents.

Ford did not timidly leave one bun firmly gripping the old wall of rationality, for the sake of an easy retreat. He boldly took both cheeks out into the meadow, and then fought to save his backside with every tool he knew. This full-fanny approach to creativity encompasses the best of what we need to reignite in America --- the drive to be great. "But how", you may ask yourself, "do I get to that point myself?" I'm glad you asked.

167

You zip up your equipment
& make a choice to enter the fray;
on a quest for Greatness

The Quest for Greatness

There was a crusty old Dane named Kierkegaard, who wrote a book called <u>Purity of Heart Is to Will One Thing</u>. Don't read it. Honest. It's so dry it'll give you dandruff. But the points he makes are terrific, so you really ought to read it. Darn. What to do? I know. Why don't I tell you about it. That way I look smarter than I am, you get the knowledge, and Kierkegaard gets the footnote, right here.[2]

Commitment

"Put your hand to the plow and don't look back."
"Keep your eye on the prize."
"Full speed ahead and damn the torpedoes."
"Purity of heart is to will one thing."

Pick your cliché. They all say the same thing. If you want to succeed, you have to be so committed that nothing, not even death itself, can sway you from your course. Very heroic, but a tad bit overblown. Frankly, most decisions aren't worth dying for. However, the general spirit of the clichés is right on target. Creativity is long hard work and it must be fueled with the kind of commitment that enables you to do what Henry Ford did - keep jumping and/or destroying hurdles.

How do I get committed? You could act very strange around your relatives. That's one way. But we're talking about a different kind of commitment here, so try the following, instead. Draw a staircase with 5 steps. Then write something you want to accomplish on each step - putting them in descending order - with the most important thing on step number 1. And don't read any further until you do.

168

1. _____

2. _____

3. _____

4. _____

5. _____

Now that you've done this little exercise, let's discuss it. One of the important discoveries of research on motivation and commitment is that attention is the key element. We tend to pour our energies into the things that are uppermost in our minds. So commitment takes care of itself, if we have our priorities in order. That's where the staircase exercise comes in. If you're like most people, your staircase will look something like the one below. The order of the top three steps may be different from one person to the next, but the broad contents usually aren't. That's very normal. It's also very interesting, because there is a clear dichotomy between steps 3 and 4. The top three priorities are outcomes, what we get. It's not until we get down to step 4 or 5 that most of us think about the inputs, what we give in order to earn the top 3 steps.

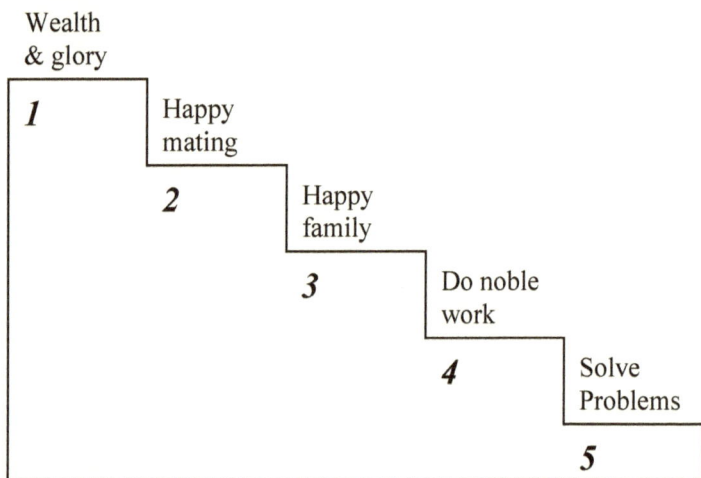

Wealth
& glory

1

Happy
mating

2

Happy
family

3

Do noble
work

4

Solve
Problems

5

If this is true for you, don't get depressed or guilt ridden. Just welcome yourself to the human race, and realize that most of us get the cart before the horse. When we try to get creative we clutter our thinking with the rewards or punishments that might result from our efforts (the outcomes) rather than pouring our attention into the effort itself (the input). Our priorities get reversed and we put two roadblocks in the way of our own actions. First we make ourselves tense, start to second guess ourselves, and start to worry about how we can manage the risk. Second, we get so busy planning our acceptance speeches or excuses, that we clutter our brains and use up the space that could be used to generate brilliant ideas.

The key to commitment, therefore, is getting your priorities straight.

Concentrate first on "what you can do", and let "what you might get" take a back seat for now. Obviously, our favorite in this book is the current occupant of step 5, "solving a problem". That's because this is a book on creativity. If it were a book on productivity I'd probably champion the current occupant of step 4 "doing good/noble work". So don't try to lead your entire life based on problem solving. Just realize that when you're trying to be creative, its a pretty good priority to have as number 1. And when you're trying to lead the rest of your life it's a good idea to follow the general rule …

focus on what you do, and let what you get take care of itself.

Immersion
Any good evangelist tells his congregation to delve into the "Word"; to study scripture to the point where the entire text becomes one long memory verse. Michelangelo advocated becoming one with the marble you carved, and Thomas Edison said that if you want to invent a light bulb you had to learn to think like electricity. Creativity requires that you immerse yourself in the subject matter. Live it. Breath it. Love it. Invite it to your bed. You can't get the insights you need by standing neatly at arm's length. You have to let the subject sweat all over you. And that's not always a pretty sight. Creative people tend to be obsessive when they're on a roll.

171

How do I get immersed? Short of becoming a Southern Baptist, immersion is an act of will rather than water. Let's take a look at some useful advice.

1. **Focus on what you love**. That way immersion works <u>with</u> your natural urges, rather than fighting them. Besides, life is too short to force yourself into something you hate.

Fred was a case in point. He was a very bright guy. He was committed to being creative. But he was worse at it than anyone I'd ever met. Eventually I found out why. He hated his job. He hated the business he was in and couldn't wait to get home each night and escape into his hobbies. And Fred was the President of his own firm. But Fred was a rare bird. He took the risk and got out. He sold the business lock stock and barrel and decided to make a living with his chief hobby, building doll houses. His creativity suddenly blossomed. He applied the notion of panelized homes on a miniature scale and offered hobbyists customized creations that were actually mass produced. Now Fred's happy. He lives and breathes doll houses, and while you may think it's a little weird to talk seriously to a doll, Fred is making about three times as much as he did acting like a grownup. Which leads us to the second point.

2. **Recapture the child in you**. Robert Fulgum wrote a book called <u>Everything I Need to Know I Learned in Kindergarten</u>. There's a lot of truth in the title. After kindergarten, the biggest thing we work on learning is how to be adult. We stop talking to dolls. We stop making crowd noises as we swing a bat behind the garage. We stop entertaining the obsessive daydreams and fantasies about what we love so that we can get to the serious business of becoming an adult clone. And to what purpose? The only thing that happens is that we become large, unhappy children who force themselves to sit in the corner. Now, before that starts to sound like a tantrum to you, let me hasten into my doctoral garb and cite some very adult empiricism to back it up.

Abraham Maslow was a very interesting psychologist. He decided to study well adjusted and highly successful people, instead of the pathologically troubled souls that most psychologists studied. The result was Maslow's famous "Hierarchy of Needs" that you probably had to memorize to get through Psych 101 in college. You'll remember that the top step in the hierarchy was "self-actualization", which - if you read the material that supported Maslow's hierarchy - is little more than a return to childhood. Self actualized people are so successful and so secure that they can openly return to the fantasies, obsessions and joys of their childhood. Period.

When you focus on what the child in you loves, immersion will take care of itself. This is my sneak attack. The act of will required here is nothing more than willing yourself to relax. Loosen that grownup tie and girdle. When you relax enough to find the child, you become a more productive adult. Don't you love it when the first chapter of a book is still relevant 185 pages later?

Focus

Let's say that you receive a divine calling while you sleep. God shows you that the acre of hardwood forest behind your house, at $1.97 per board foot, would bring in $189,000 ... enough to send all three of your kids to college and provide a very comfy retirement. You awaken with commitment, you grab your axe and immerse yourself totally in the sweat, smell and wood chips of the task. But after three solid days of incredible toil you become discouraged and quit, all without felling the first tree. Why? Because you were using the blunt end of the axe instead of the blade.

Intensity is a wonderful tool, as long as it's not wasted. But most people do just that. They get so caught up with the grand vision that they forget to focus on the details. The minor details, such as which end of the axe head you use, can make all the difference in the world.

How do I get focused? My son David was taking a Karate class. I dutifully sat and watched the class, and I noticed an interesting transformation. Back before the class, when he was trying to emulate the general mayhem that made "Teenage Mutant Ninja Turtles" such a favorite, he was a whirlwind of spastic motion and no lamp was safe. Now that his instructor had taught him the art of self-control, David focused on the precise angle of each joint, the choreographed elasticity of every move, and the attention to every detail. The lamps at home were perfectly safe, but I became a little worried about my knees. Question: How can you and I capture that same attention to detail?

1. **Make a list**. Break every task into its simplest component parts. That's what an instructor does. They don't teach you the *coup de gras* move right off the bat. They teach you how to breath, how to stand, how to hold your right hand, and how to move in rhythm with the rest of your body. And only after a year of that do they reveal the joy of using your hands as power equipment.

So make a list, and take it to the level of absurd minutia - pick up the phone, dial, talk, put down the phone, etc - because that's where you'll make some pretty amazing discoveries. Like the fact that most phone solicitors spend 80% of their time doing everything but delivering the sales pitch. So you invent the auto-dialer, increase their productivity by an exponential factor, and make life truly a pain in the neck for the rest of us.

2. **Keep notes**. We laugh at the eccentrics that walk around with a pocket full of notes scribbled on napkins and scraps of paper. But that social faux paux is okay, because they're laughing at us. They know what they're doing with their lives, while we haven't got the foggiest notion ... because we can't remember all the little insights and mental notes we generate.

So carry note cards or napkins in your pocket, keep a pad or tape recorder by the bed. Then use the darn things. If you're no longer worried about being an adult clone, they'll improve your creativity and productivity as well.

Rumination

A number of firms and nations had tried to build a canal across the isthmus of Panama. And they had all failed miserably. Every time they finished a section, the torrential rains would wash all the dirt back into the canal and return the land to the status of shallow swamp.

To combat this, the builders invented increasingly bigger steam shovels and dug ever deeper and wider trenches. But the bigger the shovels got, the bigger the subsequent landslides became. Their shovels, which were the biggest in the world (and as large as skyscrapers) did nothing more than bankrupt the enterprises with technological wizardry. In fact, at one point Panama held more heavy equipment than all but three nations on earth, and all of it was rusting from disuse. Then, in 1905, Teddy Roosevelt appointed John Stevens as the canal's project chief and the world's largest engineering project was finished in an historical blink of the eye.[3]

Stevens' success lay in the fact that he ruminated. He focused his attention on the problem itself, while everyone else wasted their time focusing on solutions.

Now there's an odd thought isn't it? The best way to get a solution is to ignore it. That goes against the very fiber of our bottom-line orientation. We want to be like John Wayne:

sashay into town, size up the problem in a split second, generate a quick solution, shoot somebody (anybody will do as long as they bleed), and ride into the sunset with the girl. Very forceful. Very quick. Very satisfying. But very ineffective.

As you study the problem itself, and roll it over in your mind, you start to see it in context. Once you do that you'll start to see solutions that already exist in other settings. It'll feel like divine revelation. But its simply the art of "contextual thinking".

That is exactly what Stevens did. He simply ruminated. And in the process he cut to the obvious, which was that he had a whole lot of dirt where he didn't want it; which meant that he needed to put all that dirt somewhere else. That's it. The success of the entire venture rested on what any 3 year old in a sand box knows.

> *The success of the Panama Canal rested on redefining it as a transportation problem, not as a digging problem.*

Stevens built a *new* wall of rationality around the concept of canals, and thereby unleashed a new set of innovations. His engineers came up with a perpetual motion train with movable track that hauled the dirt to distant swamps, where rain storms wouldn't cause a problem.

That's an amazingly simple solution; but Stevens still deserves the credit because it is so hard for adults to remember what was so obvious to us as kids:

1. Take the time to roll around in the problem itself,

2. Control your urge for an immediate resolution.

Luther redefined the situation facing him
  - ➤ from how best to obey God's law
  - ➤ to how best to accept God's grace

Franklin redefined his world as well
  - ➤ From living under the divine right of kings
  - ➤ To living in a world of equals

Smith took a look at his world and moved
  - ➤ From training man to be a moral member of society
  - ➤ To constructing a world in which man had no choice but to behave as one – regardless of where his heart lay

And Einstein turned the world on it's ear by moving
  - ➤ From a physical world driven by linear, mechanical rules
  - ➤ To a metaphysical world in which time bends and space is in a hurry

How do I learn to ruminate? All you have to do is ask yourself variations of three simple questions:

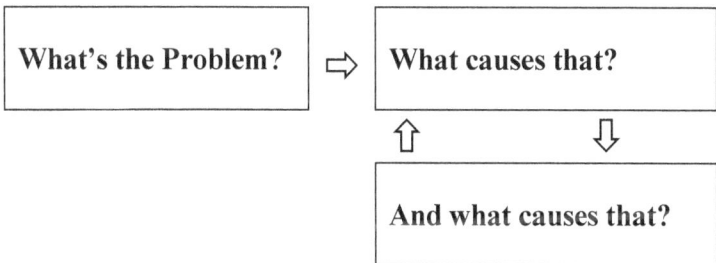

What's the Problem?	⇨	What causes that?

⇧   ⇩

And what causes that?

The tough part is that you need the discipline to ask those same questions over and over and over again; until you get to the "ninny answer" that shows up at the bottom of our example. At that point the solution will usually fall into your lap. Just remember to discipline yourself, or you'll never get beyond a superficial quick fix.

- Now, to cement this for you, take out a sheet of paper and try the same exercise on a real problem you're facing today.
- I'll give you 2-to-1 odds that the effort will get you a whole lot closer to a useful solution than you are right now.
- Go on. Take the gamble and do it.
- The worst that can happen is that you might discover the meaning of life.

What's the Problem? _____

_____

What causes that? _____

_____

And what causes that? _____

_____

And what causes that? _____

_____

_____

And why is that important ?_____

_____

Is that really true? _____

_____

Why is that? -_____

_____

Are you sure? _____

_____

1. What's the problem?	The canal is a failure.
1b. Is that really a problem?	Yes - without it freight rates are exorbitant and military transport is too slow to do any good.
2. So, what causes problem #1?	We can't keep the canal free of dirt.
2b. Is that really a problem?	Yes - we have to have a depth of 75 feet or big ships can't use it.
3. So, what causes problem # 2?	We can't dig the dirt fast enough.
3b. Is that really the cause?	Hmmm. Maybe not. The rain will catch us no matter how fast we go.
4. So, what's the real cause?	Aha! Maybe the rain is washing our dirt piles back into the canal.
4b. Is that really the cause?	Come to think of it, yes. Look out my window. It's happening right now.
5. So, what causes problem # 4?	We pile the dirt in the wrong place.
5b. Is that really the cause?	Well just look at it, stupid. It just sits there on the rim of the canal, just waiting to be washed back in. Of course it's the cause.
6. So, what causes Problem 5?	We never thought of a way to move it elsewhere. Geez, it's really a transportation problem, isn't it?
6b. Is that really the cause?	Don't be a ninny. Of course it is. Now fix it.

Gut-Check Time

You've just had Full-Fanny Creativity for lunch.

➤ For appetizers you had the strategies for coping with reality.

➤ The entre was a medium rare cut of hybrid greatness.

➤ Taken together, they provided a diet of pure meat.

➤ By this time you should be well fed and rarin' to go.

➤ But before you do, you might like to consider our dessert cart.

➤ We're serving structure au gratin and a little humanity under glass.

Endnotes

1. *The Henry Ford Story can be found in* Financial World, *August 22, 1989, p.54*

2. *Kierkegaard, Soren,* Purity of Heart is to Will One Thing, *New York, Harper & Brothers Publishers, Harper Torch Books, 1948*

3. *David McCullough,* The Path Between the Seas, *(Simon & Schuster, 1977*

4. *Those of you who are fond of academic journals will notice that my concepts of commitment, immersion, focus and rumination are similar to the concepts of intensity, persistence and choice that are the mainstream definition of motivated behavior. I prefer my own, since I think they're closer to the mark. However, since they were stimulated by someone else's work, let's cite those sources:*

5. *Weiner, B. (1980),* Human Motivation, *New York: Holt.*

6. *Churchill, Gilbert A., Neil M. Ford, Orville C. Walker Jr., (1979), "Predicting a Salesperson's Job Effort and Performance: Theoretical, Empirical, and Methodological Considerations," in* Sales Management: New Developments from Behavioral and Decision Model Research, *R. P. Bagozzi, ed., Boston: Marketing Science Institute.*

This chapter has focused on the creative process, which is a very serious topic. So serious, in fact, that in academia they'd call it something like -"The Theoretical, Empirical and Methodological Considerations of Human Motivation: A Paradigmatic Process Approach to Innovation" -just to let you know exactly how serious it is. I like my title better.

17
WALL VAULTING
(OH, WHAT THE HECK --- LET'S TAKE THE LEAP)

We have a number of problems that press on society from all directions. They constrain us in the present. They threaten our future. And they make marvelous playgrounds for the folks that want to be creative. That's a crucial point, because impact is what makes creativity worth learning. Otherwise it's just a parlor game.

I'm going to share some ideas with you, and then we're going to take a close look at how we respond to ideas. Before I do that, however, you need to know something about me. I am an old Teddy Roosevelt Republican. I've been a Republican my whole life, and tend to be conservative in my private habits and views. Normally, that's none of your business, but it will become very relevant because of some of the things I am about to say.

Energy

We live and die on electricity. But the two chief fuels that generate it, coal and petroleum are going to run out one of these days. In the mean time they are blackening our sky, creating global warming, and melting the polar ice caps – with who knows what result. The problem has now become undeniable.

The question of course is what to do about it. The 2007 Noble Prize went to Al Gore for his work on Global Warming, <u>An Inconvenient Truth</u>. Indirectly then, the Nobel Prize went to the concept of self-denial, the idea of doing with less, sacrificing personal desires for the greater good, the good of the larger community, the good of generations yet to come. It is noble in it's precepts and requires only that we change the nature of man. And it is that one little sticking point that dooms Gorism to ultimate failure. The Nature of Man does not change. Never has. Never will. We are what we are. Any system that assumes otherwise will fail.

Gore's point, of course, is that <u>this</u> time the need is so dire that man will have to change his own nature, or go extinct. In the short run (ie – the next 50 years) Gore's approach may in fact be the way to go, but only as a transition phase, while we switch to a new long-term solution.

In the end, however, man will always want more, not less - faster, not slower – louder, not softer. That is the nature of the beast. So we've got to look for a solution that works with the beast, not against it.

Until nuclear energy switches from fission to fusion, it's not going to be very popular. It does have a bit of a safety issue, plus there seems to be a downside to its by-product. There's also gasohol, natural gas and sunshine. There's also the wind, and every river could be damned. There's also hydrogen technology. But notice that every potential solution depends on some outside source of energy. We're looking at the problem from an outside-in perspective.

Why not use one of our techniques and look at this from the inside, out. How could we, personally and individually, make the electrical system of a nation self-sustaining?

You may not realize it, but that was Edison's original intention. Instead of sending out vast quantities of electricity as a finished product, your local utility was envisioned as sending out a much smaller quantity as an intermediate product. Then each consumer would use that little bit of energy to produce their own finished product, as much electricity as you wanted.

- Each building would have its own personal generator, fueled by the central utility.
- We'd get just enough power to run our personal generator, which in turn would produce much more electricity for our own use.
- Each personal generator would then contribute a few volts back to the central utility to keep it generating the next wave of intermediate energy.

Theoretically, such a delivery network could produce an endless and self-sustaining stream of energy once it got started. Think about that for a moment. It would change more than your light bill.

- Imagine the impact on electric companies. The current stress on production capacity would evaporate. In fact, their current capacity would be sufficient to handle population and industrial growth into the 22nd century.

- The utilities, or other enterprising entrepreneurs, would make a fortune on PG (personal generator) production, installation and maintenance contracts. A mammoth PG industry would spring out of nowhere and become the dominant item at the stock exchange, dwarfing anything the computer industry had ever accomplished.

- Breakdowns would affect only one house at a time. Blackouts and brownouts would be a thing of the past, because you could always borrow a "cup of electricity" from your neighbor. Repair costs could be billed directly to the needful individual rather than allocated to unaffected users. And consumer groups would die of attrition and the utilities would have a free hand.

Then look at larger society. Endless energy would finally be a reality, and world politics would go up for grabs. No one would give a rip about what the Saddam Husseins of the world did to each other, defusing the Middle East as an international hot spot. Arabian economies would go belly up and they'd have to sell their acquisitions back to the original owners just to stay afloat.

And when you stop to think of it, one little briquette of Kingsford charcoal could start the whole thing in motion. All you need is enough energy to make the initial volt. Creativity can change the course of history.

Sewage

We're running out of ways to store and treat the stuff, and it will only get worse as population increases. Science has given us a hand by coming up with constantly improved methods for breaking the stuff down into its smallest components, neutralizing the molecules and disbursing them as far away from one another as possible. But as good as those methods are, they can't keep up with population projections. So what do you do?

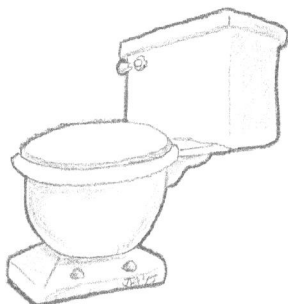

You use reverse logic and go the other way. Instead of disbursal, think about aggregation. Hoard the fecal brew, toss

185

in some enzymes, put a lid on the mix and cook it. You know what you get? Methane. That's what you call a personally renewable energy source. Think about it.

- Every day your family is flushing away enough energy to fuel the family car.
- Methane cars would be affordable since they can use the same combustion principle that applies to gasoline engines.
- A methane car runs just as fast as a gas eater, so no one has to give up their current addiction to speed.
- After the initial expense of a septic processor unit in your back yard you'd never have to stop for fuel unless you left town.
- When you were out of town, you could pull up to a prison, state hospital or public school ... which would finance themselves as energy stations instead of being a tax drain.

Now this is an idea with bite, because the motivation is based on self interest; cost savings without any loss of speed or independence. It's also pretty weird. But only because it violates the decorum within the wall - nice people don't discuss fecal material. And they certainly don't collect it for fun and profit.

Global Economics

Your world changed radically within a single 18 month period. NAFTA, GATT and the EEC created an alphabet soup of trade treaties that saw to that. Barriers have fallen left and right, and while a brave face was put on the nation's new-found opportunities, most of the populace was frightened by the fact that our first major export seemed to be jobs. Consequently, in a reprise of Rome and her water wheels, the major debating issue in America for the past few years has revolved around the best defensive strategy.

186

We need to rearrange our mindset. Let's use the obvious allegory of football and let old Bear Bryant speak to us from the grave. "The best defense," he rumbles "is a good offense." Let's start by aggressively exporting one of America's finest products - labor unions.

Yes, you heard me correctly – I'm suggesting that America go into the business of championing labor unions – and me a card carrying Republican.

The President could certainly open the gate by sliding one or two phrases into trade treaties. And the Commerce and State departments certainly have the contacts. Besides, America is such a wealthy consumer that developing countries would probably allow their own unions to prosper in exchange for hopping on the American gravy train.

The U.S. government could send over American labor advisors, drawn directly from our own unions. That kind of support and respect could pull disaffected labor leaders back into the political mainstream and give them a stake in making American economic policy work. It's always nice to turn an adversary into an advocate.

And here's where the cycle gets rewarding. If the wages in Bangladesh rise to American levels, where would manufacturers run for cheap labor? Jobs would stay at home, and American voters would be very happy. And all those high paid Bangladeshees? They'd become a glorious new market for American exports.

Then there's the effect on terrorism. The guy who's most likely to blow up a building is the one who doesn't own one of his own. The union becomes a counterweight to both the ruling family and the religious zealots of Saudi Arabia. It's a classic repeat of Richard Nixon's policy of triangulation. And as the unions eventually enable the average Islamic peon to become a property owner and thereby join the middle class, his willingness to throw a bomb disappears. Now he's got something to lose. So he becomes more careful than angry, because he now has an address --- and I know it.

Congress would certainly win brownie points from its blue collar constituents by funding the entire movement as a form of directed foreign aid. And if the Republicans were smart, they'd turn the political scene on its ear by sponsoring the whole thing in the spirit of aggressive capitalism, thereby stealing one of the Democrat's few identifiable constituencies. Voila! The captains of industry get the level playing field they profess to want. Jobs are retained in America. Domestic wages hold steady or rise. Congressmen get easily re-elected. And the Republicans get to be the party of <u>both</u> management and labor. Let the Democrats keep the unemployed. Not a bad day's work, huh?

Investment
For the most part, American's don't invest. They speculate. Consequently, they don't give a rip about dividends, or the

management decisions that lead to them. They only care about the stock's price the next day.

That makes for very peaceful stockholders' meetings - since most don't even send back their proxy votes - much less, attend. But it means that every publicly held firm is in constant danger of being sold, lock, stock and barrel, on the morrow. Merger mania comes in waves. And draconian cost cutting measures, such a massive layoffs, are the preferred management tool because they're an easy way to bolster profit over night. As a result, loyalty and dedication have gone out the window.

- If I'm a stockholder, there's no reason for me to give a rip about the people in the firm or what they do, because I'll unload the stock after the next quarterly report.

- If I'm an employee, my resume is never out of circulation. One foot, and half my attention, is always planted outside the door because you and I both know my job will probably be eliminated tomorrow. I can't even fathom the fantasy of retiring from the first firm I joined. So anything I do is aimed at making an immediate splash, so I can use it to get a better job. No one is making a long term commitment or making the kind of personal commitments that only start to bear fruit 5 years down the road.

- And if I'm management, there's no reason to show a bit of concern on either side of the fence, because they'd both just as soon slit my throat as salute. So I'll negotiate a golden parachute and suck up to my firm's competitors on the cocktail party circuit.

That doesn't exactly sound like the kind of atmosphere that nurtures long term economic health, does it? It does trigger a lot of creativity. Unfortunately, very little of that creativity is focused on making firms or products any better. Instead it's being misdirected into protecting "my" fanny, or frying the other guy's for dinner.

How do you turn that around? Easy. You realize that creativity, not to mention industrial health, is a long term investment - not an instantaneous crap shoot. Then all you do is require that investments be investments.

You pass a law which requires that all stocks must be held by the buyer for at least 5 years.

People still have the freedom to wheel and deal. Stock brokers still stay in business. Deal making remains alive and well. There's just one little change.

Everyone has to live with the results of their deals, at least long enough to suffer or prosper based on what the stocks are all about - ownership of a firm that's supposed to make a long term profit. If the dividend is your only source of income for the foreseeable future, you just might care about the business and the folks who work there. You might not be quite so cavalier about butchering the lives of employees, or so passive about the strategies and tactics of management. Who knows, that kind of attention and stability might just re-ignite the kind of loyalty, productivity and useful creativity that turn a firm into an industrial giant. Feel the adrenalin? Ain't this great?

The time-share lifestyle
America does not live here anymore. In fact there is no here, here. Husbands and wives, if they have bothered to officially wed prior to making babies, are usually on the road, due to

jobs, community involvement and personal development activities. The kids have so many activities outside of the home that they are rarely there either. And when one party is at home the rest of the "family" is more often than not, not. It is no wonder that infidelity runs rampant. We have enough data to choke a pachyderm on two income families and infidelity. It is one of the highest correlations we have in social science data. We're just not supposed to talk about it in the current political climate. And for the kids, we have drug use, gang membership and sexual behavior at a young age that all have consistently robust statistics.

We could bemoan these behaviors as signs of the continued slide in America's family values …. or, we could acknowledge what is standing right in front of us in plain view. These behaviors are actually proof that family values are alive, well and pulsating in America. It's just that our institutions are no longer relevant.

Marriage and the nuclear family are obsolete ideas. They may have been the proper social institution in the days before cars, phones, computers and whatever technology surfaces between now and the moment you read this. Marriage and the nuclear family traditionally defined a group of people who were genetically linked and unable to get away from each other. Now, we not only can get away from each other – we must. Modern society demands that we learn to live our lives separately from the people that used to be the core of our existence.

We love the mobility and adventure of all this motion and freedom. But we hunger for the intimacy of the identity bonds that traditional marriage and family gave us. So we create an unofficial patchwork family. Sally is my official bride, but since she lives in Boston, she only functions as my wife three nights a week. Sara and Sonja, in Dallas and Seattle split the other 4 nights between them, in keeping with my travel schedule. I've been living this arrangement for the past 11 years and in every respect but one Sonja and sweet, sweet Sara are every bit as much my wife as is my darling Sally. We own property, we do dishes together, we raise kids and pay bills together. Three separate households. Three loving relationships. And all hell will break loose the day Sally finds out. Or when Sara does. Or Sonja. Especially, Sonja. She knows judo.

Similar scenarios go on with the kids and their patchwork of school, church, gang, drugs and sex. Each of us is living a patchwork life – because the old institutions are no longer relevant or fulfilling.

That's where the time-share lifestyle comes into play. We recognize the new reality, legitimize polygamy, and set in motion a new culture that embraces the new arrangements rather than denies them, and provides a central mechanism for brokering, assembling and nurturing these newly permissible, and official, time-share relationships – for wives, husbands, brothers, sisters – even in-laws.

Okay, ok, ok - - - Let's dial it back

Chances are, at least one of the ideas I just rolled out caused you to wince, swear or wave the bullshit flag. If not, I'll be happy to roll out a few more. The point is that creativity does that to people. It makes them wince and swear. Why is that?

1. Creativity is change, and change is the act of letting go of one thing so you can take hold of another --- which is fine, unless you're comfortable with the thing you've already got

192

in your hand. And most people are, no matter how much they complain about it. The devil you know is better than the devil you don't know. Uncertainty is the thing we hate most in life.

2. The other thing about change is that someone is always worse off after it occurs. In divorce, one of the spouses is always worse off after the split, regardless of how miserable things had been. Of course, one of the spouses is also better off --- a lot better off.

3. The third thing about change is that it is always negative at first, for everyone. Nothing is ever where it used to be, where it's "supposed" to be. It's true of budget allocations, resources, tools, silverware --- you name it. Life just ain't the same and we're all off kilter for a while until our systems get used to the new world order.

In short, our old way of life dies every time someone in the vicinity is creative. This is especially true when we aren't the change agent ourselves. So it turns out that grief is the most useful model for coping with creativity. Years of clinical research have shown us that grief progresses in 5 clearly discernable steps. People's reaction to change (and therefore their reaction to creativity) follows the same path.

The Grief Cycle
The first response is usually "Did I hear that right? That can't be right. No. That's absurd. Who could think such a thing? That's just stupid!" This is usually the symptom most associated with paradigm shift – we simply deny the thing that stands right in front of us.

```
┌─────────────────┐          ┌─────────────────┐
│                 │          │                 │
│     Denial      │   ⇨      │      Rage       │
│                 │          │                 │
└─────────────────┘          └─────────────────┘
         ⇧                            ⇩

         ⇧                   ┌─────────────────┐
                             │                 │
                             │   Bargaining    │
                             │                 │
         ⇧                   └─────────────────┘
                                      ⇩
┌─────────────────┐          ┌─────────────────┐
│                 │          │                 │
│   Acceptance    │   ⇦      │   Depression    │
│                 │          │                 │
└─────────────────┘          └─────────────────┘
```

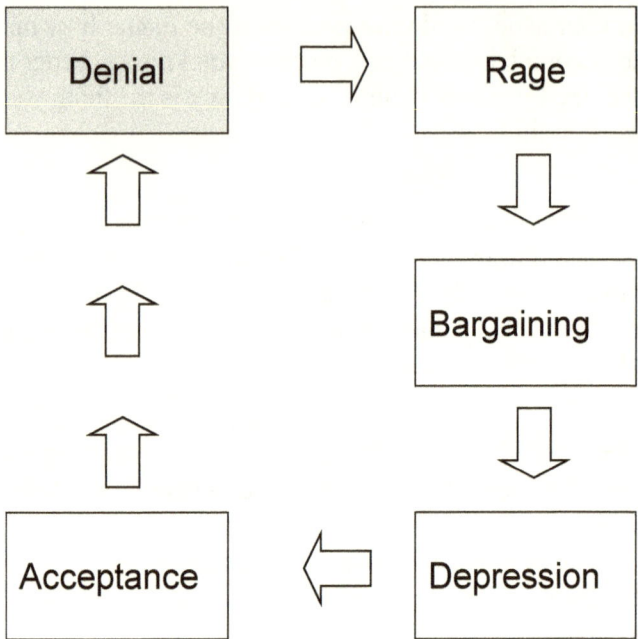

When it sinks in, the next stage unleashes various stages of
rage; from cold calculated resistance plans and pledges to
yelling and picketing. A gun is usually a great comfort to
someone in this stage. Bombs also bring peace of mind. One
wonders if the Muslim world is simply suffering from all the
technological and economic changes that have occurred in the
past 20 years. Perhaps the best way to fight terrorism is to
teach the Arabs what the Indians and Filipinos know and let
them have the concession for outsourced computer work.

When you fail to shout down, cow, or kill the source of change,
you eventually try to reason with it – you know – bribe it.
We'll even make a deal with cancer "If you let my Mom live,
I'll become a Sunday School teacher". In fact, if Al Qaeda
survives long enough, the world will eventually negotiate with
it. It is inevitable. Look at how we have made
accommodations with Iran and North Korea, despite enormous
saber rattling between 1980 and 2007.

Regardless of how successful our bargaining goes, we can never get change to disappear. Once the genie is out of the bottle, it simply refuses to go back in. As a result, depression always sets in as we deal with the fact that nothing will ever be exactly the same. We'll moan a little and cry a little, and tell nostalgic stories about the way things used to be – back in the day when life made sense and people had moral fiber. And then we'll grow quiet and stare off into the distance.

Then after a while, the new nonsense starts to become familiar. Then it becomes the norm. And eventually we accept it and start to lead a vibrant life inside the new reality. If we're lucky we'll get a few good years of that before some other jerk comes along and vomits some new "creativity" all over our new shoes. And then we're right back in the stew, moving from disbelief to rage and on through the cycle again. And again. And again.

If you're the change agent – realize that this is going to happen, to some degree, every single time you broach a new idea. And the reaction will be stronger, and the cycle time longer, the more creative you have been. That's why organizations, cultures and religions usually change <u>very</u> slowly. On the other hand, technology can change with breathtaking speed because atoms don't have a grief cycle. Of course, the scientists who study them do, as Einstein found out.

So even if you're a physicist or chemist, you'd be well served to anticipate the grief cycle and plot a strategy for plodding your way through the resistance you will encounter. And realize that while the attacks and criticism will be very personal, it's not really personal. They simply hate you, and fear you, as an agent of Satan.

If you're NOT the change agent – realize that your reactions may have little to do with the merits of the idea. You may simply be racing through the grief cycle. As a result, you may want to temper your response and not slaughter the messenger. In fact, I would go so far as to suggest the 9 Commandments of Coping with Change.

1. Agree that everyone here loves the <u>(church, company, country, faith, party, whatever. YOU fill in the blank.)</u> to the same degree. Even more important, a benevolent providence loves us all the same. When we forget that, we start sounding like politicians at election time.

2. Never call names, or cast aspersions, or turn the discussion into personal spats. That kind of behavior is an obstacle to resolving the problem and makes you look like a thumb-sucking 8th grade brat. How's that for name calling?

3. Never assume that you know the other guy's motivation. Only he can tell you what that is. The best you can do is take his word for it.

4. Wait for your turn to talk. Then be brief.

5. Listen to what the other guy actually says. Most of us don't listen. We're just marking time, waiting for the other guy to take a breath so we can counterattack.

6. Focus on the functional, not the moral point of view. No one compromises on morals. Once it becomes a moral issue the only possible resolution is the other guy's death (or yours).

7. Look for common ground. Shared values, vision, goals give us a place to start.

8. If tempers flare, separate and take a break—with the promise to return to the table, at a specific time.

9. Discipline yourself to say "My, isn't that fascinating. Why do you think that?"

These commandments are nothing more than Franklin's guidelines for civil discourse. Ignore them, and you won't be able to compromise. And if you can't compromise, you can't govern, you can only dictate. Chaos ensues and everything starts to implode. Once you've called someone a nigger-loving, rug-munching, pinko, running-dog, honkie, dike, ass-bandit, himmie infidel, camel jockey it's hard to say "Now, how can we resolve this little disagreement?" Words, my friend, are bullets. Once you send them out, you can't say "Oops! Do over!"

That's a point we've forgotten here in America. We've always been a cantankerous lot, but our current lack of civility started with Rush Limbaugh back in the early 1990s. He was an entertainingly rude conservative pundit who delighted his audience with the crudest labels for liberals (things like the "Femi-Nazis" who loved to pass the tampon of authority). He became so popular that every radio station wanted him, and when they couldn't all get <u>him</u> they turned to the likes of Neal Boortz, Glenn Beck and Sean Hannity; each one vying for the title of most obnoxious in defense of "the American Way". As a result, we now have a complete generation of adults who couldn't have a civil discussion about getting a drink of water. The only thing they know how to do is call names and holler "leper!" This garbage has to stop folks. We have created an environment in which it is not safe to have an idea. Now I ask you, in all candor --- how is that different from the most restrictive Muslim village? You've seen what that mindset has done to their culture. Is that what you want for your own?

The ideas that led off this chapter may change the course of history. Then again, they may not work at all. In fact, they may prove to be absurd. But I love this country no less than you. In fact, I wish only to make it a healthier, happier, more fulfilling place to live --- as do you. I may find your ideas to be just as lame. But unless I talk to you, and you to me, I will never fully grasp the two seeds of genius that sit within your mental oatmeal, and you will never see mine. And since we'll never compromise, all of those seeds will be lost for generations to come.

The Muslims have fallen behind the rest of the world technologically because they have remained militantly rigid in their opposition to new ideas. How odd it is that a culture that once ruled so much of the world, and was the keeper of human knowledge during the Dark Ages, should have fallen so low – and done so by it's own hand.

I do not wish for America to follow that same path. Consequently, I have decided not to hit you when you have a new idea. I hope you will do me the favor of a similar response

> … or I will remove your liver with a dull spoon and feed it to the dogs that surround the town dump, with their running sores and ulcerous tongues (may they drool on you forever).

18

THE "S" WORD
(WASHING IN THE WORD WHICH MUST NOT BE SPOKEN)

Most "how-to" books don't tell you how to handle success in their particular area of expertise. It's as though they don't want to jinx things by talking about success ahead of time. I think that's balderdash.

I prefer the approach of Ray Morris, my high school football coach. The day before our first game, he took the team over to the bench area on the game field – old Russ Bullard Field. "Gentlemen" he intoned, "We have worked hard. We are ready. We are going to arise victorious tomorrow night. In fact, we are going to rampage our way to victory every night this season. So the eyes of Florida shall be upon us.

It is therefore of paramount importance that we comport ourselves (he was from the deep south where they love such words, delivered with extra syllables on each vowel) it is of paramount importance that we comport ourselves as champions both on and off the field."

For the next 30 minutes he did a humorous but meticulous tutorial on how to conduct oneself on the sidelines. How and where to run off the field. How and where to run onto the field, so as not to encumber the gentlemen coming off the field. Where to sit, where to stand. Where to look. Proper topics of sideline conversation. Who got to stand close to the coach, and in what order. Who got to say something directly to the coach and who had to relay their comment via someone else. And after the inevitable victory, how to talk to reporters, who to thank, what to say, how to say it, where to look, and what not to touch while on camera.

In short, he was showing us how victory would feel and taste and smell. Did talking about victory jinx us? We lost a heart breaker the next night ---- but, we won all the rest and ended up Conference Champs. So all in all, I think talking about success ahead of time is a good thing.

What exactly is Success?
In general, success is the functional completion of whatever task you set your mind to; turning a page, tying your shoes or creating new life forms on distant planets. Specific to

creativity however, we'd have to be a bit more detailed. Success in this endeavor means

1. getting past the old wall
and
2. building a new one out in the meadow.

It's a two-stage process. Getting outside the old wall is only half the battle. If you don't build your own walled enclave out there, then you haven't really created anything, have you? All you've done is run away from something.

- At best you're just a talented outlaw, whose chief joy is thumbing his nose at anyone who tries to tell him what to do.
- At worst, you're the village idiot who's just doing a random walk through the daisy patch.

Creativity, remember, is a quest for the next undiscovered tidbit of Natural Law. That's one of the things we learned up on the mountain top.

When does success occur?

That depends on you, really. It can't occur before you're done. Up until then you're simply "in process." So how do you know when you're done? Well, how do you know when you've gotten to Albuquerque? Is it when you cross the city limits, or when you get to city hall?

- On the one hand, you're done, when YOU say you're done. You came up with the task, after all. You set the goal. You, therefore ought to be the judge of when you've accomplished your own goal.

- On the other hand, maybe the general public is the best judge. Franklin did not succeed as a stove designer until he came up with a design that the general public bought in droves, making him a millionaire. Of course, the same was

also true of his invention of lightning rods. Every building
on the American continent had at least one Franklin rod. At
$2 a piece, he was a millionaire all over again. Or his
bifocals, which half the population over 40 depended on.
Yikes, there's another million.

• On the third hand, if you're keeping count, maybe success
awaits an anointing by the experts. Einstein was not a
success until the scientific community admitted their
inability to disprove his theories. And his big moment
came in 1919 when an impartial 3rd party used a total
eclipse to confirm that the light bouncing off the planet
Mercury behaved exactly as the General Theory of
Relativity predicted it would.

How far can I go --- Out beyond Success

Success is all well and good. But there is so much more to be
had. Success is simply the validation of an accomplished task
in the here and now. When the general populace takes you to
their bosom and loves you for it, that success becomes fame.
And if that fame lasts beyond the generation of your children,
then congratulations, you have attained glory. And if they
still remember your name 2,000 years later, and if they still
tell tales of your life, your struggles and victories, then
congratulations my son --- you have become a legend.

Adam Smith has glory; but Luther, Franklin, and Einstein ----
now they are legends. Wouldn't you like to do something
with your life that is worthy of being a legend? I sure as heck
hope so. Otherwise we've both been wasting our time.

Here it is

In a paraphrase of Ray Morris, allow me to say, "Folks, you
are going to succeed. You've worked hard. You've learned a
lot. There is no further preparation you can do. Trust your
instincts. The force will be with you. You will succeed. It is

therefore of paramount importance that you comport yourselves as true champions, cognizant of victory's taste and smell and all it entails. So tuck in your jersey and listen up"

How will I respond to success?

That depends on your motivation for being creative in the first place.

		Need for Truth	
		High	**Low**
Need for Wealth and/or Glory	**High**	I **am** the mouthpiece of God	Eat your heart out, punk
	Low	It works! That's kinda neat.	What's next

That was actually a trick question. The whole mountain-top half of the book drummed home the message that Creatives are driven first and foremost by the need to discover & promulgate "Truth". Therefore their need for Truth is uniformly high. Of course, the mountain top view also drummed home the fact that going over the wall requires an ego the size of Texas. So the need for wealth and/or glory is also uniformly high, if for no other reason than self justification. Consequently, all four of our mountain top guests sit firmly in the upper left quadrant – seeing themselves as the mouthpiece of God.

- Luther, of course is obvious in this, since it was just him and God doing battle side by side against the evil Pope and his minions.
- It is also evident in Smith's books. It drips from his imperious and condescending pen.

203

- Einstein explicitly used himself as the benchmark of what a rational and clever god would have thought and done, and
- Franklin expended considerable ink writing instructions to his son on how to be the messenger of all-knowing providence without triggering resistance from his audience.

So the true Creatives all clump together in one quadrant. I see. You have to have **a balance** between your hungers for Truth and Glory. Hmmm. Then, who in the world occupies the remaining 3 cells?

Columbus is the classic example of someone who occupies the upper right quadrant. He obsessed over wealth and glory, and had only mild interest in Truth. As a result, his reaction to his own success was an openly trash talking, in your face "told you so" smack down, which established the incredibly cruel form of governance of Spain's new world colonies and landed Columbus in chains as an abrupt end to his tenure in office. Success brought out the beast.

Paul McCreedy was a good example of someone in the lower left quadrant: an innovative guy with a high commitment to truth but a low need for wealth or glory. His response to success was pleasure, not joy. Success simply confirmed an earlier hunch (I thought so!). He may represent the best of creativity in the trenches.

Jedidiah Barlett, Nobel laureate, President of the United States and a completely believable figment of someone's imagination is the classic example of creativity gone empty. He inhabited the lower right hand quadrant. The political deals necessary for attaining and keeping political office extinguished his quest for truth, and the brutality of political in-fighting replaced the quest for wealth and glory with the struggle for survival. So throughout the entire West Wing

204

series, his most repeated line was "What's next?" Success was simply a bus station on the way to the next disaster.

Can you still be creative _after_ you succeed?

Up until 1919, Einstein was a house afire. Creativity erupted from him in a constant stream. Then the eclipse convinced even his most ardent adversaries, and one of those flukes of history occurred.

The world turned Einstein into an international celebrity. He did a world tour to deliver lectures about relativity, and pandemonium broke loose wherever he showed up. Crowds in the hundreds of thousands jammed the docks to watch his ship pull in. Two hundred thousand would stand in the rain outside some massive auditorium that sat only 20 thousand. They would stand for hours just to listen to the loudspeakers and catch a glimpse of him. Reporters would send each other to their deaths fighting for space on the waterfront gangplanks. He was bigger than any king, any actor, any pope. And his fame continued for the next 35 years. He was a phenomena – which is one step beyond a legend in the short run. Only time will tell his significance in the long run. Although he did win TIME magazine's "Man of the Century" designation, which is a hopeful indicator that he will remain a legend for centuries to come.

There was just one little glitch. His creativity dried up in 1920. Well, actually, let's just say that at age 40, he stopped producing the incredible breakthroughs he had produced before age 40.

That triggers a gut-check question in my mind. Is the same thing gonna happen to me, when I succeed? That's a pretty sobering thought. What if the one thing you depend on and glory in suddenly disappears?

Before you consider suicide as the only rational next step, pause to ponder a moment. The undiscovered world will not have disappeared (except for the one thing you just discovered). In addition, there is no evidence that success kills brain cells (except for the ones knocked off by a week of celebratory binging). So there is no functional reason why you shouldn't continue to be as creative as you desire. In fact, it should be even easier to be creative.

- You'll face less resistance
- You'll get more cooperation
- More people will volunteer information, insights & results
- You'll get financing easier for labs, experiments etc.
- It'll be far easier to get your stuff published
- You'll have more self-confidence
- You'll have a broader perspective, with bigger targets.

And the list goes on. And on. That stumped me until I realized that the very trappings of success may be the enemy of ongoing success. Creative success is the same as political, commercial, financial, athletic and any other type of success. It turns you into a celebrity, and celebrities always get an entourage – a group of hangers-on, who bask in your reflected glory and become groupies – professional yes-men, playthings and gophers. They look like a sounding board, but they're not. It's your fame they love, not you; and they're sycophants, not people who will lovingly disagree and push you a little now and then.

Creativity requires resistance. That's what keeps you focused.

If there weren't a wall to rail against, you'd never have the energy or the gleeful desperation. The fire in your belly would dissipate in the absence of a clearly defined foe. Without the wall your fanatic zeal turns into mellow confidence, your intellectual hunger turns into appetite. Your initial success makes pursuing the same old task kind of boring. And in the absence of the wall, only one thing stands between you and intellectual drift --- your sounding board. Luther, Franklin and Smith kept theirs throughout life – Franklin going so far as to put together the American Philosophical Society so that he could have a sounding board of sufficient talent to keep up with him.

Einstein, however, moved away from his – both physically and emotionally. Maurice Solovine's expertise in philosophy was no longer a part of his everyday life. Conrad Habicht's mathematical expertise was also missing. Einstein kept up a life long correspondence with them – but never again did he have that kind of daily in-your-face feedback from folks who truly loved him.

Keep a strong sounding board readily at hand.

The Turf Trap
Success entails building your own, new, wall out in the meadow. All well and good, unless you make the mistake of assuming that your wall is any more sacred that the wall you left behind. The moment that happens, you get trapped.

Because from then on you've got to defend <u>your</u> wall. If you don't, truth goes down the drain, along with your reputation and your disciples (ie – entourage) as well. No more invitations to A-List parties. No more evenings in the Lincoln bedroom at the White House. At the extreme, no more mentions in the history books. Playing defense wears you out, and puts no points on the board. Luther and Einstein started playing defense in middle age and therefore didn't add much new material after that. Franklin, on the other hand, never assumed he'd found <u>the</u> final answer to anything. Consequently, he never wasted any time playing defense. Which is probably why he was still being incredibly creative at age 90.

Put Truth before Ego, or you can kiss creativity goodbye.

Creativity is like a passing game.
It's only good on offense. Passing is worthless on defense. In fact, it's impossible. Offense and defense require different skills, different attitudes and different aptitudes. In his hay day, Einstein used his Jewish Science as an offensive weapon – his weird stories were central to discovering new things, uncovering truth, creating compelling proofs. In the process he overcame the essential concept of Newtonian Physics – absolute time and space – and thereby unlocked the door to relativity.

After 1920, however, Einstein started to use his stories (thought experiments) to debunk anyone who threatened his own wall, and stopped using them as his primary tool for discovering new truths out in the meadow. For that, he relied almost exclusively on mathematics, the tool he had disdained during his prolific period as a crutch for people too scared to think for themselves.

Use your best tool on offense
not defense

Getting off track

Einstein obliterated Newton's sacred cow – absolute time and space. But he brought his own sacred cow with him - absolute and discrete prediction and measurement. Then Einstein created his own worst nightmare – quantum physics.

Quantum Physics turned out to be dependent on mushy probability predictions and measurements because it deals with quanta, which is both a particle and a wave, and you never know exactly where one of those little buggers is going to end up. Not only that, but in Quantum Physics, the very act of measuring reality alters reality, except for the fact that reality only exists when you do measure it. Go ahead and reread that, slowly.

This was just too much for Einstein and he spent 35 years trying to debunk what his mind simply could not accept. I imagine that God was chuckling the whole time. Again, sometimes success plants the seed of subsequent problems. The law of unintended effects – change always leads to more change.

So there was Einstein, still one of the sharpest minds on planet earth, spending a good deal of his last 35 years blowing up imaginary cats, then poisoning them, melting them and disintegrating the poor little felines, in a hilarious series of thought experiments with another scholar by the name of Erwin Schrodinger - all in an effort to disprove a theory he himself had created then couldn't fully understand. Imagine if he'd used that wasted time on something else. Turns out, he did.

Launching the grand quest.

Sometimes success allows us the opportunity, and gives us the confidence, to try something that mere mortals have the good sense not to even attempt. Einstein was such a guy. His top most scientific passion in those last 35 years was to develop a general field theory --- a singular explanation for all the phenomena in the world – from the very small to the incredibly enormous. Now that's what you call a life calling. On several occasions, he seemed to have come within a hair's breadth of doing it. But he never got there. Or maybe he did. The story goes that on the night he died, he suddenly cried out "I have it" then rattled off a detailed explanation of something or other, but his nurse spoke no German whatsoever. So the secret of the universe, if he'd found it, died with him. He however, died with a smile on his face.

Use your success as a launch pad from which to pursue the impossible

Changing your Focus

Success allows you the leisure of moving from Gnostic to Nephish. You no longer have to be compartmentalized. You can step outside your box. The #2 thing on your "life list" gets to move up to #1, once you've successfully dispatched the old #1. Franklin's incredible wealth from being a tinker (stoves, swim fins, lightening rods) gave him the ability to step credibly into the forefront of scholarly work on electricity. Smith's success with moral sentiments, paved the way for his work in economics. And Einstein's fame as a Scientific celebrity gave him the credibility to become a political force to be reckoned with.

- He was a leading voice in the pacifist movement that followed WWI, popularizing the 2% solution --- through which, just 2% of those drafted could cause a war effort to collapse simply by refusing to serve.

- He was subsequently a leading voice that helped kill that same pacifist movement when Hitler rose to power.

- He remained a strong international voice for socialism his whole life,

- he raised prodigious funds and public opinion favoring the creation of Israel. And

- he was offered the presidency of that nation once it was established.

- In addition, he was instrumental in getting the bulk of Jewish physicists out of Germany and into the United States prior to WWII, which not only was the deciding factor in us developing the atomic bomb, not Hitler – but also gave the US a leg up in the race to the moon.

- And it was Einstein's personal letter to Franklin Roosevelt that triggered the start of the nuclear age, the day after Roosevelt received it.

Maybe, just maybe, success doesn't do a bit of harm to creativity. It just allows us to play it out in vastly different ways. **I** may be disappointed that I don't have the secrets that Einstein coulda, shoulda, woulda discovered. But I'll bet you my bottom dollar that Einstein wasn't.

He led his life exactly the way he wanted to. He didn't let folks lock him in his lab at Princeton and force him to be productive out of some trumped up guilt-debt the gifted are supposed to owe society. The President of Berkley tried exactly that. As did the head of the Institute at Princeton,

211

where Einstein finally settled. Even Eisenhower, war hero and President, failed to get Einstein to "buckle down and turn out some more knowledge".

SO ...

❖ Give yourself permission to succeed
❖ Describe what success would be
❖ Admit you want it
❖ Fight for it
❖ Acknowledge your successes openly
❖ Don't shy away from them
❖ Don't undersell them
❖ Take a moment to bask in them
❖ Then ask yourself what <u>you</u> want to do next
❖ Do not (repeat, <u>NOT</u>) ever let others put you in a box

I think Ayn Rand may have had it right, in <u>Atlas Shrugged</u>. I also think John Galt would have liked <u>this</u> book. Get to know him, and let me know what you think.

❧

19

THE LAST BLAST

(A CLOSING COMMENT)

I figure that if you're still with me at this point I can tell you some things about vision-based leadership that might have scared you away in Chapter 1. The first of those things is my answer to a question I get from people when they first consider vaulting over the wall ...

Will I Get Weird?

You bet. The Wall of Rationality is the boundary of normalcy. By definition, anything that lies outside it is non-normal and therefore weird. So if you play with the non-normal out there in the meadow, it rubs off. Maybe you're just being creative when it comes to finding a new way to store paper clips. But beware. The mindset and method you use in that quest will start to seep into the rest of your life. You'll start to ask similar "what-if" questions about other tasks at work and home. You'll soon start to see that a lot of other tasks could be improved. But those are outside your purview. No one asked you to redesign dishwashing at home. No one asked you to revamp the entire R&D function at work. They simply wanted you to untangle the paper clips, for god's sake. What's gotten into you?

You've just bumped into a major source of tension in organizations. Most executives tend to fantasize that creativity can be compartmentalized, and turned on and off at will. That way it gives its "good" stuff (new ideas) to the organization without upsetting the apple cart, or any of the apples that lie therein. Managers fantasize that a creative person should dress and act just like everyone else, perceive the world just like everyone else, and have the same values as everyone else. So at the same time that managers are encouraging people to be creative, they also tend to discourage them, because they squash any attendant behavior that's outside the norm. In short, many executives demand that their employees vault the wall without really vaulting the wall. A track coach who tried that approach would be fired as a health hazard.

If you're getting depressed and wary as you read this, take heart. My wife disagrees with me. She says it's entirely possible to be very creative without getting weird. As an example, she cites herself. She has been a successful executive for years, has an eye for finding novel approaches to building relationships and solving problems, and (she claims) she is still the epitome of normalcy and decorum. She bathes regularly, wears grownup clothes, conducts herself with charm and grace, and is loved and respected by all who know her. How much more normal can you get?

The fact of the matter, however, is that she's about as weird as they come. Her kids glow in the dark, because the only home cooked meals they had for 22 years came from the microwave. She can't remember how to make a bed. And even her underwear is "dry clean only", because she doesn't do laundry.

She's so weird that she's turned her back on everything a woman was created to do and be.

Now don't throw a fit and burn the book. There's a serious and crucial point to be made here. When you get creative, you don't just vault the wall and wander aimlessly out there in the meadow. You either move the old wall or build a new one ... especially if there is a bunch of you being similarity creative at the same time. Then something interesting happens.

> The old wall of rationality that surrounded the concept of womanhood said a woman had to cook and clean and nurture children, not business ventures. But after a generation of womanly "weirdness", that's no longer the case, is it? The definition of what it means to be a good and useful woman has changed, hasn't it? At least in public. Someone moved the wall.

The point of all this is as follows. **Being creative will make you seem weird at first. But as your "weirdness" continues, the rest of the world will catch up to you and you'll no longer be considered weird.** In fact, at some point in the future, you may even be seen as an old stick-in-the-mud traditionalist.

The moral lesson here is this: stop wasting time trying to fit in.

We all get a little goofy when we're being creative, and even when we're not, we still look a little weird to the folks back inside the old wall. Accept it. It's the price of making your mark in the world. It's also a badge of honor. As George Bernard Shaw said,

"The reasonable man adapts himself to the world; the unreasonable one persists in trying to adapt the world to himself. Therefore, all progress depends on the unreasonable man."

The great thing about the wall of rationality is that it's moveable. You can enlarge it. You can transport it. You can take it apart and haul selected bricks out into the meadow to help build a new wall. It's just very heavy, so movement is slow. It never occurs fast enough when it's our idea. But it alters the face of the world because it sends history down a different course than it would otherwise have taken.

And it always - I repeat, <u>always</u> - starts with a single individual. Maybe I'm that person. More likely, you are. I firmly believe that one of you will change the face of manufacturing, inventing new products and processes that make my life easier. One of you will finally unlock the cure for cancer and remove the scourge that claimed my brother in his youth. One of you will redesign the educational system. One of you may become Pope and alter the course of religion. And one of you may be President ... right now. If so, Mr. President, I'd be honored by the opportunity to talk things over.

The individual is the crowning glory of creation and the veritable engine that drives society down the road to progress. Yet it's easy to lose sight of the individual in today's world, where everything seems to revolve around the group. It is especially tough for the individual to get his due in this day and age because we live in a world of false modesty. Steven Jobs (the founder of Apple Computers) and Bill Gates (the founder of Microsoft) are two of the few creative people who happily blew their own horns, and a lot of people didn't much like them for that very reason. Society prefers to see the self-effacing genius who always gives the credit to someone else. That's why the world was so comfortable with Johan Sebastian Bach, its most prolific composer. He started each composition with the invocation, "God grant me the wisdom", and ended it with "Sola gloria Deo" (To God, alone, be the glory).

But don't get side tracked by Bach's statements. They were not false modesty or the result of a diminished self image. You see, down in his gut, Bach knew that he was the only one God spoke to with this extraordinary message of music. He therefore knew his importance as an individual, and he knew the importance of honing his skills to the peak of their potential.

That's where a book like this comes in. Whatever your endeavor, wherever you need creativity, this book has given you the tools to reach the peak of your potential. The only thing that remains is to chat a bit about change, and offer some last advice and a pep talk.

We Live In A World of Change

Now here's a comforting thought - that great idea you had last year is probably obsolete. At the very moment you are reading this section something is occurring in a laboratory, or out in the field, or in world events that will change the world so radically that the knowledge you have at this very moment won't be enough to cope with the new situations you'll face. For example, when I started writing this book:

Only two geeks in California knew who Bill Gates was, Ronald Reagan was President and Pope John Paul II was a vibrant middle-aged man. The internet was a tedious but useful way for academics to send binary code to one another.

"Russia" still meant the entire empire of the USSR instead of its largest republic, the iron curtain was still firmly in place, and the Berlin Wall was a functioning wall not a series of concrete billboards or souvenirs.

The Savings and Loan industry was still considered a viable financial player, not a $700 billion albatross around the nation's neck.

Drexel Burnham not only existed, it was one of the most feared, envied and admired financial houses in the world.

American Motors was an independent company, not a subsidiary of the Chrysler Corporation. And Chrysler Corporation was an independent company, not a part of Daimler-Benz (so now it's back to being independent anyway). Sometimes change can't make up its own mind.

Cigarette smoking was not the mark of Cain.

There was no Amazon.com or eBay, and people got their books the old-fashioned way. They borrowed them at the public library. And if you googled somebody you were literally baby-talking.

George W. Bush was a lightweight party boy living off his Dad's contacts and spending most of his time at the ballpark.

People still ate junk food and babies still wet their diapers.

In a few short years, most of that changed. Thank goodness for soggy diapers. It's nice to know that some things are eternal. The point is that the world will continue to change, and if you're trying to use last year's techniques in the 21st century, you'll be in trouble.

The world that lies before us will be different than what we face today - markedly different. And the changes will come from several different places. Let's look at just two.

Technology

Think about superconductivity and genetic research. Those two things, alone, promise to change the way life is lived. Then add holographic projection and the next logical step, molecular transfer ... and leaven it all with computer technology that seems to expand at an exponential rate. You know what you'll have? A little bit of Star Trek. Within the next 20 years you just might be saying "Beam me up, Scotty", instead of hailing a cab. By the year 2050 you might just have to go to a museum to see an airplane, and automobiles might just be a silly looking relic. Transportation, as we know it, would have ceased, and "dropping in to pay a visit" would have a whole new meaning. In fact, Harry Potter's flue dust might be a viable transportation technology. No one has a crystal ball, but I'll bet you my royalty check that breakthroughs of this magnitude are just around the corner, and they'll change more than just the way we do business.

Culture

For a moment, imagine that genetic research discovers the DNA strand that triggers aging, and controls it. That one technological change, by itself, will turn culture on its ear. Imagine if your great, great grandfather were still alive and healthy. What a joy. What a sense of continuity and family. And what an obstacle to change. Imagine conducting your current courtships according to the rules of 1923, because great, great grandpa is still head of the clan. Imagine the collapse of the social security system and the resulting financial panic. Imagine holding a dance party in your home with great grandpa aghast at the pelvic undulations of the modern age. And what in the world would you do as a marketer?

If age no longer meant sickness and senility, and if age continued to command some sense of deference and status; what would that suggest for the cult of youth that has dominated so much of American production and marketing?

Would the Pepsi generation suddenly become tennis players over the age of 90?

A Little Advice

If you want to succeed, and have an impact on the world (and your wallet as well), I have four pieces of advice for you.

First - learn to go against your own human nature.
Back in 101 B.C., the Romans discovered they could use water power to run its mill wheels. Pause a minute and think about the impact of that discovery. Prior to hydro-power each mill wheel had required a crew of 10 guys to keep it working. There was about one mill wheel for every 1,000 people. So, given the population of the day, almost a quarter of a million millers were suddenly freed from mindless drudge work. That was a quarter of a million brains that could be directed to better pursuits, and a half million hands to bring those plans to fruition.

But in the short term, it meant a quarter of a million unemployed millers, and pushing 4-ton mill wheels around every day had made them very strong ... and scary. So instead of retraining that army of laborers - thereby helping both them and society - Rome opted for the quick fix and outlawed the water wheel to avoid unemployment riots. And that was the way things stood for 400 years, until Emperor Constantine was forced to reintroduce the water wheel, due to a lack of slave labor. In the meantime, Rome had deprived itself of twenty generations of potential scholars, mechanics and generals. No wonder the empire collapsed. It's stupid to try to prevent change. Yet history shows us, time and again, that stupidity is often our first reaction. Why?

Progress - whether it's new ideas, machines or processes – requires that we fight our hatred of change. You'll want to monitor and combat that gut of yours. Make peace with discomfort and realize that creativity is an endless process. First you come up with a new idea. Then you enjoy it. But then you have to get creative all over again to clean up the unanticipated problems your first brainstorm caused. That leads to another cycle of ideas, enjoyment and cleanup ... and on and on it goes. Creativity is a real pain in the neck. Or maybe it should be seen as a self-sustaining historical process. I prefer the latter view.

Second - place a high premium on knowledge.

It is the real fuel of industry and, like any other energy source, it's important that knowledge be cheap, abundant and readily available to an economy's organizations. But sometimes we get in our own way by destroying it, ignoring it, or outlawing it on moral grounds. The results can be disastrous.

Julius Caesar burned the vast library at Alexandria during his march through Egypt. Very impressive. And also very tragic, because that one act of political machismo put humanity behind the 8-ball. The library at Alexandria had been the world's single biggest repository of scientific knowledge, and it took almost 1,000 years to re-discover and re-invent all the knowledge that Cleopatra could access with a library card. That millennium of ignorance is what made the Dark Ages dark. It may also be the reason why Edison made the first light bulb instead of Michelangelo, and why the Wright Brothers made the first flight instead of Columbus.

George Bush Sr. loudly blocked fetal cell research in a desperate attempt to suck up to the moralistic right wing of the Republican party. And my own brother was one of those who died because progress toward a cure was delayed until after Bush lost the election to Clinton.

When David was 8, I found out that I'm in the same league with Caesar and Bush. In a fit of parental ire, I threw out a pile of papers and other junk that had been cluttering his room for the past 2 months. Then I made him stand beside me to watch the garbage truck drive away with his treasured stuff. As it departed, he squeezed my hand in sympathy, and informed me that my computer manual had been in the midst of all his clutter. I worry about a kid with such a well developed sense of humor.

Here's my point. Even though breakthroughs are the product of one person's mind, they are usually based on the knowledge accumulated by others. So anything that destroys knowledge, or makes it off limits, delays or destroys human progress.

Support for education is a crucial part of any approach to knowledge, since a good general level of knowledge in the populace is necessary for the development and operation of technology.

But creativity has little to do with the general level of education or knowledge of the masses. Instead, it's based on the genius of individuals, and the opportunity to let that idea have its day in the sun. So while you're making those sizable endowments to your favorite university, don't forget that the most important support you can give the store house of human knowledge is the simple act of listening to an employee (or even someone walking in off the street) when they tell you an idea, and then giving them the opportunity and resources to see if it works.

The third piece of advice is, have courage.
Market research will indicate disaster for just about any new technology because there's no way for potential users to knowledgeably judge it.

> Walt Disney almost went belly up in the 30's because banks refused to lend him enough money to complete "Snow White and the Seven Dwarfs". They had very impressive

research which clearly showed that no one would pay money to see a feature length cartoon.

IBM took a grand leap of faith in the main frame computer market back in the 50's in spite of extensive research which indicated that the total market included no more than five - get that, only five - potential customers in the whole world.

Obviously, someone in both organizations had the courage to press on despite "traditional wisdom" (which is often just another way to say "coward's folly").

The final piece of advice is - Embrace serendipity.

Ivory Soap, that wonder soap that floats, was the vehicle on which Proctor and Gamble rode to world prominence. And it was a mistake. Some bozo in the mixing room fell asleep at the switch and let a batch of their old soap be mixed far longer than prescribed. The result was a frothy mess. But when it solidified .. voila! Marketing history was made. All that froth dried into air bubbles, and Ivory became the first floating soap.

That little bit of magic would have been lost, **if** someone at P&G had not taken the time to see what serendipity had dropped in their laps. Think of it as cooking pasta. Before you throw away your mistakes, you might just want to heave them against the wall and see if something sticks.

Which brings us to the 3-M company.

Its research and development folks were looking for a high strength industrial grade adhesive that was easy to handle, and they came up with a test batch that was an utter failure.

- It was easy to handle, alright, because it had all the holding power of an arthritic grandma. Like most other development failures is was earmarked to become toxic waste.

- But one creative soul decided to try something before pitching the abortive batch. He slapped a little on the back of his secretary's phone message sheets and reassembled the stack. She loved it and the result was another profitable little tidbit of marketing history - POST IT note pads.

- Although it has an "of course" quality now, the mental transition from laminating building materials to reminding your spouse to pick up the dry cleaning is a grand leap, and it all came from a bad batch of glue.

- It occurred because someone trusted their gut, not their research.

The Simple Tasks in Life
As useful as creativity is on the grand stage of world politics and economics, don't ever forget that it's equally as useful on the mundane tasks of everyday life.

- You can change your fortunes in courtship by redefining the situation. Instead of a grand hunt, make it a dance.

- You can improve your effectiveness at work by learning to relax, working smarter rather than harder.

- You can improve your relationship with your kids by taking an inside-out approach to the problems that arise.

A Final Farewell

(A pep-talk for Americans)

There have been two hidden players in this book - von Clauswitz, and Asia. Old General von Clauswitz wrote that war led most nations into one of two traps: (1) using the weapons and tactics of the last war, or (2) copying the opponent's tactics in the current one. The first trap is one of obsolescence. The second is one of stupidity. Your opponent is better at their own tactics than you could ever be, and they've had time to figure out ways to counteract them if need be.

And that leads us to Asia: especially China, Japan, India and Korea. The Japanese are great managers, with a higher ability to manage communal efficiency than our culture allows us to have or exercise here in the States. The Chinese have seemingly unlimited raw materials and manpower. India does have unlimited manpower – and a vast number of them have been educated in our best schools. No nation understands what makes the US and Great Britain tick as well as India. They are the vast sleeping giant. The Koreans have proven engineering skills, and together, the Asian cultures tend to have a willingness to sacrifice individual gain for communal gain, which is definitely NOT an American trait.

As a result, Asia can beat us on price and take enormous chunks of market share --- if we let the battle be fought on the battle ground of efficiency. We fell into that trap back in the 80s with the Japanese. They kicked our butts for almost a decade. To our credit, we worked our way back into the game, but never did more than hold them off in a stalemate. Then the dot.com era dawned and we swamped the Japanese by leap-frogging past their finely tuned technology. Nobody cares about the world's best buggy whips when there are no more buggies.

Yet, U.S. firms are falling back into von Clauswitz's second trap – trying to beat the opponent with their own weapons and tactics. In other words, we're letting the opponent decide where the battle is fought. That's why we're back to our old love affair with cost cutting efficiency – including shipping jobs to New Delhi, Mexico and the Philippines. And it will lead us down a deceptive spiral - going broke ever more efficiently.

America isn't real good at efficiency over the long haul.
- We're big, noisy, sprawling, brawling, self-centered individualists who get sloppy and wasteful.
- We lack the tradition, taste and culture that the rest of the world takes for granted, and we are often our own worst enemy.
- We hardly ever agree with each other, and it seems like we're always jockeying for position in some strange political game of one-upsmanship.

In fact, the only thing going for us is that we seem to do two things better than anyone else.
1. We're a bit more willing to bash through the wall than others, and
2. ultimately, we aim at effectiveness more than efficiency …when we put our minds to it. So, if we want to hold our own in the future, we might want to change our tactics and build on what we do best. It goes back to the core of American business culture: good old Yankee Ingenuity, the search for effectiveness, which requires equal parts creativity and courage. And all in all, that's not a bad combination.

So …

Go be wonderful at something.
It doesn't matter what.
Just be wonderful.

You now have permission.

In the doing, you will become a leader,
because you will know where B is.
(And that is what vision-based leadership looks like.)

Sola gloria Deo

The Author - *Joe Anderson,* PhD

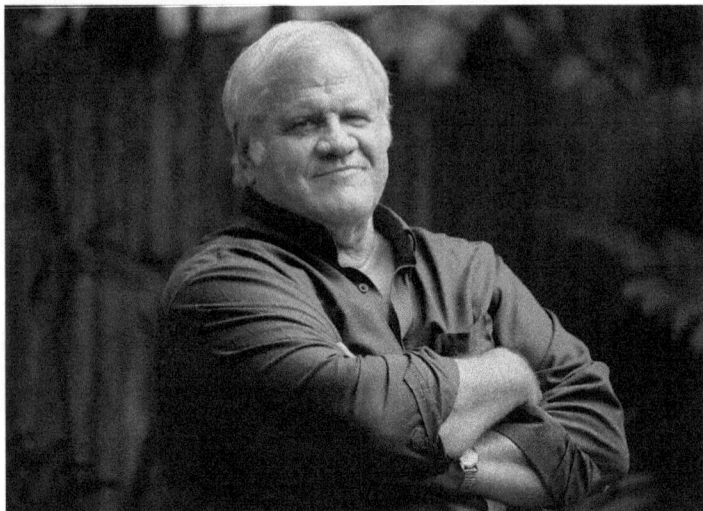

Joe has served as personal advisor and counselor to more than 60 CEOs, controlling over $8 billion a year in sales and 3,500 employees - in large measure, via his chairmanship with Vistage - formerly known as The Executive Committee (TEC). He's been doing that job since 1995, along with occasional public speaking and a pretty fair amount of writing.

Prior to that, he successfully ran an organization himself, then went to grad school to find out why it had gone so well. He emerged with a PhD and taught for 10 years in some of the leading business schools in America; getting voted Professor of the Year at several of them. You can visit him via:

www.JoeAndersonPhD.com

Other Books by Joe Anderson, PhD

THAT THING BETWEEN YOUR EARS IS AN IDEA:
How to get one. How to use it. How to lose it when you're
done.   (Available at Amazon.com)
The average business needs a good, big, idea every 17.3 weeks –
just to stay abreast of the competition. You know --- things like
new products, processes and/or markets to pursue. But those are
hard to come by because we've hemmed ourselves in by creating
and enforcing a multitude of little ideas; like inventory systems,
budgets, performance metrics, etc. So we forget what a good, big
one even smells like, much less how to actually have one. That's
where this book comes in. It will literally jump start your brain.

http://www.amazon.com/That-Thing-Between-Your-
Ears/dp/0984712038/ref=sr_1_1?ie=UTF8&qid=1430778843
&sr=8-
1&keywords=that+thing+between+your+ears+is+an+idea

THE 4th CIRCLE: How we fall into stress & how to climb
back out.   (Available at Amazon.com)
Being in charge is the most dangerous thing you will ever do. And
it doesn't matter what, exactly, you're in charge of: church
committee, or all of General Electric. The stress of being in charge
can literally kill you. But it doesn't have to be that way. We can
uncover the prime causes of stress; and actually turn them into tools
that help us master our jobs, our relationships, and therefore … our
lives. It's not a miracle cure folks. But it *has* had remarkable
results.

http://www.amazon.com/4th-Circle-fall-stress-
climb/dp/0984712070/ref=sr_1_1_twi_1_pap?ie=UTF8&qid=1430
778910&sr=8-1&keywords=the+4th+circle

www.ingramcontent.com/pod-product-compliance
Lightning Source LLC
Chambersburg PA
CBHW022055210326
41519CB00054B/429